GUIDE TO SPIRITUAL L.A.

The Irreverent, the Awake,
& the True

For Glen,
Happy Travels!

Green Tara Press

Green Tara Press
Los Angeles, CA 90064

Library of Congress Control Number: 2020910129

Auman, Catherine I.

Guide to Spiritual L.A: The Irreverent, the Awake, and the True
1. Travel 2. Spirituality 3. Los Angeles

ISBN 978-1-945085-09-3 (paperback)
ISBN 978-1-945085-10-9 (electronic book text)

Spiritual History of L.A. by Philp Goldberg was previously published in *LA Yoga* Magazine. Reprinted by permission.

Photos on pages 78,152 and 153 courtesy of Peace Awareness Labyrinth & Gardens

Cover Photo is of the *Nuestra Reina de Los Angeles* or "Queen of the Angels" statue by Ada May Sharpless and is at Echo Park Lake, L.A., CA

Author Photo by Greg Lawrence

All photos except as noted by Catherine Auman

Book Design by Katrina Pacheco

Printed in South Korea

GUIDE TO SPIRITUAL L.A.

The Irreverent, the Awake, & the True

CATHERINE AUMAN

FOREWARD by PHILIP GOLDBERG, Author of *American Veda: From Emerson and The Beatles to Yoga and Meditation, How Indian Spirituality Changed the West*

CONTENTS

FOREWORD by Philip Goldberg **1**

GET READY TO ROLL **6**
Introduction 7
The Legend of Lemuria 8

THEY WERE HERE FIRST **9**
The Original Angelenos 10
Tour: Native Spiritual Sites 12
Where the World Began 20
Shaman, Warrior, Queen 22

LATINO SPIRITUAL L.A. **24**
On a Mission – The Catholic Church 26
A Rich Spiritual Universe 29

THE FRUITS & THE NUTS 31

THE SPIRITUAL RENAISSANCE OF THE 20S & 30S 34
Hollywood is a Powerful Spiritual Vortex 35
What are Vortexes? 36
Tour: Spiritual L.A. Hollywood 38
The Big Scary Church that isn't Frightening at All (to Visit) 41
What Does Scientology Actually Teach? 42
Yogananda and the West's First View of the East 44
Tour: L.A. Yogananda Empire 46
Jesus Came from Outer Space 50
UFO Activity in Greater L.A. 52
Aldous Was Here 54
The Huxleys in Paradise 56
The Pumpkin Bread Nuns 58
The Secrets of Krotona 60
The Theosophical Society and Bad Rockstar Behavior 63
Want to Learn the Secret Teachings of All Ages? 66
She was Sexy, She was Hot, and She Served God 68
Whole Lotta Shakin' 72
Mount Helios Love Cult 74
The Lizard People Who Lived Under L.A. 76

OCCULT L.A./THE WESTERN TRADITION 77
Tour: Eastside Spiritual L.A. 78
Nine Famous and Infamous Los Angeles Occultists 82
He Blew Himself Up, Or Did He? 84
The Wickedest Man in the World 86
The Scarlet Woman 88
B.O.T.A. 90
The Dark Side 92

TRADITIONAL RELIGIONS 94
Traditional Religions in L.A. 94
Ten Famous Churches and Temples in L.A. 98
Holy Cow 102
L'Chaim! 103
Our Newest Friends 106

SPIRITUAL AWAKENING OF THE 60S & 70S 108
Tour: Westside Spiritual L.A. 109
Father Yod and The Source Family 112
Flirty Fishing 114
"Turn On, Tune In, and Drop Out" 116
Oh Happy Day 118
Drugs, Brujos, Shapeshifting, and the Witches 121
Z is for Zsuanna 124
The Church of Synanon 126
MSIA 128
Spirituality in a Speedo 130
Answering the Question: Who Are Those All-White Turban People? 132
Inn of the Seventh Ray 134

AND A WEALTH OF OTHERS 137
The Rise of the New Religions 138
The Science of Mind 140
Tour: Midtown Spiritual L.A. 142
Madonna and the Red String Brigade 144
Mindful Masters 146
Angel Face, Angel Food 148
Maybe a Little Too Hot 150
Peace Awareness Labyrinth & Gardens 152
Arianna Huffington: Spiritual Adept 154
The School in the Closet 156
We Let, We Let it Be 158

Hare Krishna Hare Krishna 160
Westside Guru 163
Telepathic Instruction from the Masters 164
Spiritual Hipsters 166
Venice and Spiritual L.A. 168

DAY TRIPS 170
Tour: Desert Day Trip 171
Weird Scenes Inside the Goldmine 175
The Integratron 176
The Interplanetary Airport and the Come On Inn 178
Giant Rock 180
Joshua Tree National Park 181
Rock Stars, Peyote, and the Voice of an Ethereal Being 182
Joshua Retreat Center and the Institute of Mentalphysics 186
Desert Christ Park 188
Desert Hot Springs – Cabot Yerxa 190
Tour: Spiritual L.A. Day Trip East 192
Sacred Mount Baldy 194
A Frenzy of Love 195
Tour: Day Trip Santa Barbara 200
Shalawa Meadow 204
The Western Gate 206
Tour: Day Trip to Ojai 208
Tour: Day Trip South 212

ODDS, ENDS, & ECCENTRICITIES **219**
The Miss Velma Christmas Show 220
Spiritual L.A. Yearly Calendar of Events 222
Best Spiritual L.A. Movies 223
Ten Places to Get A Reading Right Now 224
Spiritual L.A./New Age/Occult Bookstores and Shops 226
Spiritual L.A.'s Best Meditation Gardens 228

Best Places in L.A. to Feel the Shakti 230
Ten Southern California Vortexes 232
Top Ten Spiritual L.A. Scandals 234
Top Ten Spiritual L.A. Badass Women 236
Top Ten Spiritual L.A. Rockstars 238

AFTERWORD **240**

ABOUT THE AUTHOR **242**

ACKNOWLEDGMENTS **244**

INDEX **246**

OTHER BOOKS BY GREEN TARA PRESS **250**

Photo right: The Lady of the Lake Statue, Echo Park

FOREWORD

SPIRITUAL HISTORY OF L.A.

By Philip Goldberg

When he first arrived on the West Coast Paramahansa Yogananada called Los Angeles "the Benares of America." L.A. reminded him of India's holiest city because a certain spiritual energy permeated the hot, dry air. He may have sensed that the growing town was destined to become the prime relay station for the processing and distribution of yogic teachings.

Yogananda himself, of course, played a principal role in that history. After making a twelve-acre site atop Mount Washington the international headquarters of his Self-Realization Fellowship, he became "the twentieth-century's first superstar guru," to quote the *Los Angeles Times*. Over the years, Yogananda's visible footprint was placed on other choice properties in the region, notably the magnificent Lake Shrine on Sunset in Pacific Palisades and the cliff top retreat in Encinitas, where he wrote his iconic memoir, *Autobiography of a Yogi*.

More than two decades before Yogananda made L.A. his home, Swami Vivekananada ushered in the twentieth century in this part of the world. During his three-month visit commencing in December of 1899, lecture halls were filled with crowds eager to hear the triumphant star of the 1893 World's Parliament of Religions speak on subjects like "The Science of Yoga." In 1923, one of his devotees, Swami Paramananda, founded Ananda Ashrama, a still-functioning sanctuary in the hills of La Crescenta. A few years later, the triple-domed temple of the Vedanta Society rose up in Hollywood. There in the 40s and 50s, a trio of celebrated authors, Gerald Heard, Christopher Isherwood, and Aldous Huxley, were schooled in Vedanta philosophy and yogic practices by the erudite Swami Prabhavananda, who presided over the temple from 1929 until his death in 1976 at the age of eighty-two. The essays, novels and nonfiction books (for example, Huxley's seminal *The Perennial Philosophy*) produced by those literary lions educated millions about India's spiritual treasures. Prabhavananda and Isherwood teamed up on elegant translations of the Bhagavad Gita and the Yoga Sutras (titled *How to Know God*) that were the best-read versions of those classics for years. The Hollywood center remains a custodian of Vivekananda's vision of adapting the ancient dharma to the modern West.

The other Hollywood – the star-making industry, as opposed to the geographical entity – has also played a major role in beaming yoga and Indian philosophy to the masses. As early as the 1930s, celebrities such as Charlie Chaplin and Greta Garbo would motor up to Ojai in their roadsters to listen to the pathless pathfinder, Jiddhu Krishnamurti. It was in Ojai that the iconoclastic Krishnamurti had the spiritual breakthrough that led him to reject the messiah-like role for which he'd been groomed by the Theosophists who brought him to the West as a teenager. For nearly six decades, his spring lecture series drew thousands of Angelenos to Ojai annually.

Hollywood star power also taught folks in the hinterlands about hatha yoga. Celebs like Mae West and Greta Garbo were linked to the practice early on, and in the 1950s, gossip columnists reported that icons such as Gary Cooper, Marlon Brando, and Marilyn Monroe were into it. Marilyn was said to do asanas "to improve her legs" proving that yoga as physical fitness did not begin in the Madonna era. One of the teachers of celebrities and thousands of others was Indra Devi, the so-called "first lady of yoga," whose landmark book, *Forever Young, Forever Healthy*, coupled with numerous public appearances, helped bring the teachings to the masses. Born in Eastern Europe, she was a student of the legendary hatha revivalist Tirumalai Krishnamachary. Only an exceptional woman could have broken through India's male-only yoga club back then, and Indra Devi remained exceptional until her death in 2002 at the age of 102.

Among the region's other mid-century hatha teachers was Bishnu Charan Ghosh, Yogananda's younger brother. One of his students was Bikram Choudhury, who went on to build a worldwide empire with his trademark high-temperature yoga. Another innovator in L.A. at the time was Richard Hittleman. A devotee of the non-dualist saint Ramana Maharshi, Hittleman penned enormously popular books and pioneered the use of video. His daily TV show, "Yoga for Health", debuted in L.A. in 1961 and was syndicated nationally for years.

In 1953, Judith Tyberg, a direct disciple of Sri Aurobindo, one of the spiritual giants of modern India, founded the East-West Cultural Center near the intersection of Beverly and Vermont. The center moved several times before settling into its present location in Culver City in 1985. A native San Diegan who studied Sanskrit in Benares, Dr. Tyberg introduced Angelenos to Sri Aurobindo's work and hosted visiting teachers who went on to have a huge impact on modern yoga. Among them was Swami Vishnudevananda, who was sent to America in 1957 by his guru, Swami Sivananda of Rishikesh. Ganga White, one of the many seekers who found their way to East-West in the 60s, trained with Vishnudevananda and later opened the Sivananda Center for Yoga on Sunset and Western during the apex of flower power. The Hare Krishna devotees added to the colorful atmosphere of the era, giving locals their first glimpse of traditional Hindu bhakti and their first earful of Sanskrit chanting, a precursor to today's kirtan scene. They would soon establish an L.A. temple (now in Culver City) and, in 1977, start their annual Festival of Chariots in Venice.

In the 70s, White disconnected from the Sivananda lineage and turned The Center for Yoga into a prototype of today's independent studio. It offered an eclectic menu of classes and hosted a parade of luminaries, from Swami Satchidananda to Allen Ginsberg to the first teachers trained by the influential hatha masters B.K.S. Iyengar and Pattabhi Jois (Iyengar himself lectured there in 1976, as did Pattbhi Jois in 1985.) The center caught on quickly, forcing a move to a larger location on Larchmont Boulevard, which is now owned by YogaWorks. White went on to found the White Lotus Foundation in Santa Barbara, and Swami Vishnudevananda's lineage was reestablished as the Sivananada Yoga Vedanta Center which is now located in Marina del Rey.

The watershed moment in the West's embrace of India's spiritual heritage came when the Beatles met Maharishi Mahesh Yogi, studied his Transcendental Meditation (TM) and, in early 1968, famously retreated to the banks of the Ganges River. Overnight, words like mantra, guru, and ashram entered the collective vocabulary, and it became acceptable, even fashionable, to start the day in silent meditation. The locus of that phenomena was London, but the sparks were lit earlier in L.A. when clean-cut citizens of Ozzie and Harriet's America were drawn to the Maharishi. When college students looking for ways to expand their awareness without dangerous drugs turned to TM, the Students International Meditation Society (SIMS) was created at UCLA. By 1966, SIMS had branches at several major campuses, and after the Beatles' media explosion its office on Gayley Avenue became the administrative engine of a massive movement. One of the UCLA meditators, Keith Wallace, wrote his doctoral dissertation on the physiology of TM, and his findings, published in 1970, would jumpstart a research juggernaut that moved meditation into the mainstream.

The chain reaction that led directly to the Beatles began with an L.A. record producer named Richard Bock. The head of World Pacific Records, Bock started promoting the music of Ravi Shankar soon after the great sitarist's first visit to the West in 1956. He produced some of Shankar's early albums and connected him to L.A.-based jazz artists like flutist Paul Horn, who became one of the first American TM teachers and later recorded the seminal *Inside the Taj Mahal* album. Bock also introduced Shankar to John Coltrane, who infused his music with Indian sounds and themes, and to Alice Coltrane, who went on to become a swami with an ashram of her own in the Malibu hills. It was also through Bock that David Crosby, then a member of the Byrds, first heard Shankar's music. Crosby shared his discovery with George Harrison in 1965, at a Benedict Canyon party. The rest is musical and spiritual history. While studying sitar with Shankar in India, the quiet Beatle's spiritual longing found direction, and his path led to the historic Beatles-in-India moment.

Once the floodgates were opened, L.A. continued to be the principal conduit for the East-to-West transmission. Yogi Bhajan, who first appeared at the East-West Center in 1969, started teaching his distinctive kundalini yoga on Melrose Ave, down the road from the Bodhi Tree, which in 1970 established itself as the prototype for spiritual bookstores everywhere. Also starting up in a Melrose storefront (circa 1972) was the American guru who was born Franklin Jones, became Bubba Free John and, after more name changes, passed away as Adi Da Samraj.

Virtually every teacher whose impact reverberated nationally made important inroads in Los Angeles. Swami Muktananda, for instance, introduced his Siddha Yoga to Angelenos during his three world tours, beginning in 1970. On his first visit, he was accompanied by Ram Dass, who was then in the early stages of his indispensable life as the spiritual teacher formerly known as Harvard psychologist Richard Alpert. Muktananda spent six months in L.A. on his third tour, holding public events in a huge tent in Santa Monica where the Loews Hotel now stands. His successor, Swami Chidvilasananda (Gurumayi), also came to Los Angeles a number of times in the 80s and 90s. And, as local yogis know, B.K.S. Iyengar and Pattabhi Jois, the progenitors of the asana-based practice now virtually synonymous with the word yoga, established a powerful L.A. presence. The transmission continued through the turn of the century, as new teachers, Sri Sri Ravi Shankar, Mata Amritanandamayi, Sri Karunamayi, Sadhguru Jaggi Vasudev, and others – have found some of their most welcoming audiences in L.A.

Somehow, a city known for glitz and glamour also acquired a strong ethos of inner development: In what other city could Bhakti Fest, Yoga Month or yoga therapy have been incubated? Where else could professor Christopher Chapple create a Yoga Studies program at the Jesuit-run Loyola Marymount University? Los Angeles has probably produced more yoga teachers per capita than anywhere else in the county, and must surely head the nation in the number of asanas performed and mantras intoned per day. By all indications, the Benares of America will continue to beam yoga in all its forms as skillfully as it beams movies and TV shows.

—

Philip Goldberg is the author of *American Veda: From Emerson and The Beatles to Yoga and Meditation, How Indian Spirituality Changed the West.*

GET READY TO ROLL

INTRODUCTION

In a land of constant seismic activity, where the ever-present threat of "The Big One" has kept Angelenos on their toes for more than two centuries, L.A. has been the birthplace of earthquakes of another kind: religious awakenings, divine energy outpourings, and spiritual realizations.

While to most of the world L.A. represents all that is superficial, deep at its core L.A. is the World Center of Spiritual Awakening, the cutting edge of as-far-West-as-you-can-go. The individuals who have relocated here, free thinkers, health seekers, and freedom lovers, have sought a spiritual understanding that was as unique as they were, often to the point of inventing it themselves.

They came here to what had already been named "The City of Angels" or, officially in Spanish, *El Pueblo de la Reina de Los Angeles*, "The Town of the Queen of Angels." Methinks it's not an accident that our beloved "Los Angeles" literally means "The Angels."

So, pull up a chair, or get in your car and be ready to tour: This book has it all. We'll travel through time, cruise up and down the coast, and head out to the desert. We'll visit people and places much to your liking, and some you'll wish you'd never met. You'll learn a little history, some philosophy, and hopefully gain a smattering of enlightenment. Come, let me share with you the treasures and delights of what we all adore: our wild and wonderful city, L.A., full of shakti and love.

THE LEGEND OF LEMURIA

A world of beautiful, healthy, pleasure-loving people; a highly advanced civilization – wait – are we talking about Los Angeles? Or the lost continent of Lemuria, also known as Mu?

For centuries occult writers have written about a lost continent called Lemuria that submerged beneath the Pacific Ocean, a counterpart to Atlantis that sank below the Atlantic. California is believed to be all that is left above water of the landmass. Some writers believe that contemporary Californians are reincarnated Lemurians, or descendants of the few Lemurian survivors who escaped to what are now known as the Santa Monica Mountains or Mount Shasta.

The great Flood was believed to have happened in 12,500 BCE when the entire Lemurian civilization was cataclysmically destroyed. Interestingly enough, Chumash legends tell of a Native people civilization in California wiped out by a catastrophic flood.

There are reportedly Lemurian ruins up by the Ventura County line surrounded by trees and foliage and hidden from the beaten path. Perhaps you and your friends will find them?

THEY WERE HERE FIRST

THE ORIGINAL ANGELENOS

On June 18, 2019, California Governor Gavin Newsom met with Native tribal leaders and issued a formal apology for the "... genocide. No other way to describe it." This was in marked contrast to the first governor of California who told the Legislature in 1851 that there would be war "until the Indian race becomes extinct." The initial governor turned out to be pretty much right: 80-95 percent of Native Peoples have been murdered, slaughtered, or killed by exposure to white diseases and the planned obliteration of their culture and heritage.

For Native Peoples, all of life was spiritual and sacred, and it was not about mastering nature but rather living in harmony with it. Each person was to honor the land and work for the good of all and not just oneself. The spiritual life was tended to by shamans or medicine men and women, and the wisdom of Elders.

The prominent tribes of greater L.A., the Chumash and the Tongva, were powerful and peaceful. Their cultures thrived in the paradisiacal climate, the abundant food, and easy trade. The Chumash lived primarily along the coast from Malibu to the Lompoc area and were known as fishermen and artisans. The Tongva, or People of the Earth, lived along the coast down to South Bay and inland to the San Gabriel Valley. They are also known by the names given to them by the missionaries: the Gabrieleños (for Mission San Gabriel) and the Fernandeños (for Mission San Fernando). Smaller tribes in L.A. were the Tataviam or Alliklik, Kitanemuk, Serrano, and Cahuilla.

Tongva names that live on to the present day include Topanga, Tujunga, Azusa, Pacoima, Cahuenga, and Rancho Cucamonga.

Photo right:
Kuruvugna

TOUR

NATIVE AMERICAN SACRED SITES AND MUSEUMS

Of course, all land was sacred to the Indigenous Peoples. These places in particular were revered, often because they were burial sites, places of power, or portals to other dimensions.

L.A. COUNTY

Kuruvugna Springs

Hidden away at University High School lies one of the last remaining sites sacred to the Tungva. The Springs are the site of a former Native village and in the 1990s were revived to use for ceremonial events. A peaceful, quiet spot -- relax and listen to the music of the stream, watch the dragonflies, check out the dwellings, or visit the museum and chat with the docents. Only open the first Saturdays of the month. Check their Facebook page to see if they're open this particular first Saturday.

1439 S Barrington Ave, Los Angeles, CA 90025

Photo left:
Tongva Park

L.A. COUNTY

❷ Puvungna

On the grounds of Cal State Long Beach. Follow the signs to the Earl Miller Japanese Garden. Park and walk behind the Garden to a clearing with totem poles (see page 21).

📍 *1250 N Bellflower Blvd, Long Beach, CA 90815*

❸ Tongva Park

We took their land; we can at least give them a park. Note several sculptures that are modern interpretations of the Tongva dwellings seen at Kuruvugna or in one of the museums.

📍 *1615 Ocean Ave, Santa Monica, CA 90401*

Wishtoyo Chumash Village

Authentic replica of a Native village and an active cultural center. Check the Facebook page for public invites to attend ceremonial events and open times for visiting.

33904 Pacific Coast Hwy, Malibu, CA 90265

Puvungna

Tongva Park

Wishtoyo Chumash Village

UP NORTH

SANTA MARIA
101
135
1
LOS ALAMOS
LOS OLIVOS
LOS PADRES NATIONAL FOREST
246
101
LOMPOC
BUELLTON
SOLVANG
CACHUMA LAKE RECREATION AREA
ARLIGHT
1
154
33
OJAI
CONCEPCION
GAVIOTA
101
MONTECITO
192
150
OAK VIEW
33
SANTA BARBARA
VENTURA
1
2
3
4

UP NORTH

1 Ojai

Native people considered the entire Ojai Valley to have healing properties (see page 208).

Ojai Valley, Ojai, CA 93023

2 Shalawa Meadow

Ancient Chumash burial site. Strong shakti. Public parking at the end of the street. Walk through the flowering lane, turn right at the beach, and walk until you see the Meadow on your right (see page 205).

Eucalyptus Ln, Montecito, CA 93108

3 The Western Gate

A portal to other realms, sacred land to the Chumash located at Jalama Beach County Park (see page 206).

9999 Jalama Rd, Lompoc, CA 93436

4 Zaca Lake

Closed. You can't get in. Or maybe you can (see page 233).

8000 Foxen Canyon Rd, Santa Maria, CA 93454

Photo left:
Kuruvugna Springs

NATIVE AMERICAN MUSEUMS

MUSEUMS WHERE WE CAN LEARN ABOUT WHO CAME BEFORE

1. **Chumash Cultural Center**
   On the site of a former Chumash village named Sap'wi. Wonderful museum, a replica of a Chumash village, and pictographs.
   3290 Lang Ranch Pkwy, Thousand Oaks, CA 91362

2. **Heritage Park in Santa Fe Springs (Tongva Exhibit)**
   12100 Mora Dr, Santa Fe Springs, CA 90670

3. **Natural History Museum of Los Angeles County (Lando Hall)**
   900 W Exposition Blvd, Los Angeles, CA 90007

4. **Satwiwa Native American Indian Cultural Center**
   26876 Mulholland Hwy, Calabasas, CA 91302

5. **Southwest Museum of the American Indian**
   Widely considered one of the largest and most important collections in the U.S.
   234 Museum Dr, Los Angeles, CA 90065

Photo left:
Chumash Cultural Center

WHERE THE WORLD BEGAN

Another place sacred to the Tongva is Puvunga, believed to be the "place of emergence" where the world began. It is the birthplace of the prophet, Chingishmish, who taught the people how to feed themselves. Puvunga is also the site of burial grounds and a formerly thriving village.

If you walk behind the Earl Miller Japanese Garden on the campus of Cal State Long Beach, you'll come to a clearing by a spring surrounded by grassy fields. There you'll find totem poles and medicine wheels. The day we visited Native people were meeting, and we spoke briefly with Anna who was quite welcoming. A little boy named Goyo was listening to us, and at one point he announced, "We are warriors for Mother Earth."

As warriors, the Tongva have repeatedly had to go to war for this land to be recognized as a holy site. Developers have tried to build a strip mall at the location, and the University has attempted to nullify their designation on the National Register of Historic Places. Most of the archaeological sites spread all over the campus have been destroyed. And, it still goes on today: in 2020 a lawsuit was filed against the University for dumping construction dirt and debris (including PVC pipe and a manhole cover) on their sacred land.

From the parking lot, if you walk in the direction of a lone pine tree and cross the road you drove in on, you'll find a circle of stones with the word Puvunga on them. When the remains of an Indian burial were found here, the body was dug up and put into a drawer in the archaeology department. When people found out about this there was a protest, and the sacred bones were buried at the circle. The spot is not marked and is not easy to find unless you look for it.

Although there may not be a lot to see at Puvunga, it is beautiful to make the trip to honor this sacred land. To stop and breathe in its rich history while standing in the midst of quiet nature, who knows? Maybe this is where the world began.

Photo left:
Puvungna

Toypurina mural at The Mural Mile

SHAMAN, WARRIOR, QUEEN

Toypurina (1760-1799) had watched the white settlers at the San Gabriel Mission steal her people's land and steadily usurp their culture since she was twelve years old. She was a powerful shaman, spiritual leader, and medicine woman known to all neighboring tribes, and the sister of the head of her village. The missions were military strongholds with a record of violence against the Native people and forced conversions to Catholicism. When she was twenty-five, the Fathers at the Mission committed what was the last straw: they outlawed native ceremonial dancing. Toypurina took action.

She used her fame and persuasive communication skills to gather leaders from six of the eight local tribes, then led them in an armed revolt against the Mission. Unfortunately, someone inside the Mission had tipped off the Fathers, and Toypurina and the warriors were captured and imprisoned. Still, this incident stands as a powerful symbol of Tongva resistance against the cultural genocide perpetrated by the Mission system.

The warriors were sentenced to a public lashing of fifteen to twenty-five blows to send a message of intimidation to all who might resist. Toypurina was punished by being prohibited to ever see her people again or speak her language – she was banished to a northern California mission, forced to be baptized, and to marry a Spanish soldier with whom she had three children. Toypurina died at the age of thirty-nine.

Scholars have variously referred to Toypurina as a witch or as a "seductive sorceress," who "used sex magic to control men." To many others, Toypurina has become an icon, celebrated on murals, cartoons, and graphics. Her life and leadership are inspiring, and she is called a Native Joan of Arc, a resistance fighter, a spiritual queen, a baddass, a girlboss. A play about her life was written by two members of the Gabrieleño tribe which debuted at the San Gabriel Mission Playhouse in 2014 and toured California in 2016.

Toypurina's legacy lives on at The Mural Mile in Pacoima. An all-women, Latina group of artists named HOODsisters created the wall-sized painting in 2014. There is also a beautiful memorial to this Native American heroine in Hawaiian Gardens.

Toypurina Memorial

Fedde Middle School

21409 Elaine Ave, Hawaiian Gardens, CA 90716

Toypurina Mural at The Mural Mile

12959 Van Nuys Blvd., Pacoima, CA, 91331

LATINO SPIRITUAL L.A.

Photo left:
Mission San Gabriel

ON A MISSION - THE CATHOLIC CHURCH

Spain's plan to steal the land of the indigenous people and bully them into accepting Catholicism was in full force in Southern California. In the eighteenth century the Church established twenty-one missions along the Camino Royale, now known as the 101. The missions were built to be about a day's walk between them and ranged from San Diego to Sonoma. The Missions' history is unfortunately an account of slavery, violence, rape, and genocide. Father Junipero Serra, the founder of the Mission project, is held up as a hero to school children, but that honorific is thankfully being re-thought. Stanford University is one institution that is erasing his name from buildings and streets.

Los Angeles County has two of these twenty-one missions: Mission San Gabriel Archangel (in San Gabriel) and Mission San Fernando Rey de Espana (in Mission Hills). The intention to establish Spanish power in the New World was of course short lived, but the plan to decimate and disempower the Native Americans was unfortunately "successful," if that is what you call it.

MISSION SAN GABRIEL ARCÁNGEL

Founded in 1771, Mission San Gabriel was the first mission in LA County and the fourth in the state. It is considered the most flourishing of the chain because of its high number of (forced) baptisms and agricultural productivity. It was built with unique Moorish-style architecture modeled after a fortress in Cordoba, Spain. The grounds hold a full Stations of the Cross believed to have been painted by Natives.

The story is that the founders of the Mission were met with a large group of armed Tongva people who were ready to defend their land from being stolen. Apparently, when one of the padres laid a painting of "Our Lady of Sorrows" on the ground, the Native people were so moved by its beauty that they laid down their arms and made peace. (Hmmm...). Today you can see this powerful painting in the Mission sanctuary.

Mission San Gabriel

Not only did the missionaries begin baptizing the Native people in earnest, they took away their name, calling them *Gabrieleños* after the name of the mission instead. The population of the indigenous people was reduced from three thousand to five hundred in a few years. There was a famous revolt against the mission by the Tongva led by Toypurina (see page 22).

In July, 2020, The Mission suffered severe fire damage, possibly due to arson. Days prior, the statue of Junipero Sera had been removed to protect it from possible BLM protesters.

Mission San Gabriel Arcángel

427 S. Junipero Serra Dr, San Gabriel, CA 91776

MISSION SAN FERNANDO REY DE ESPANA

Established in 1797, the Mission San Fernando was also on a mission to convert and conquer the Native people, and it stole their names as well, calling them the Fernandeños after the mission.

The site is beautiful and well-preserved. One highlight is the nineteen arches lining the full length of the building. Inside is an elaborate walnut altar brought over from Spain.

Bob Hope, the famous comedian and well-loved actor, is buried at the San Fernando Mission Cemetery. His grandson reported that when Bob was asked by his wife where he wanted to be buried, he answered, "Surprise me." His wife was a life-long Catholic.

Today you can visit the church, museum, gift shop, and grounds.

San Fernando Mission

15151 San Fernando Mission Blvd, Mission Hills, CA 91345
Hours: 9-4:30

Botica Del Pueblo

A RICH SPIRITUAL UNIVERSE

Hundreds of botánicas populate L.A., and most of us don't know that they are the tip of the iceberg of a rich spiritual universe. On the surface, these little shops, literally "plant stores" or dispensaries of medicinal herbs, sell items of spiritual import similar to a Catholic supply store or even a New Age bookstore with its (high-priced) candles and crystals. But when you learn the history and something of the spiritual culture, you will find them to be much, much more.

When Africans were kidnapped and forced into slavery in the New World, they were also prohibited from practicing their indigenous religion on the threat of death. As had been done before to the Native Peoples, the Catholic Church required involuntary conversions to the faith. The African people were genius, however, in melding the mystical truth of Catholicism with their own sacred practices. Their religion went underground in the Latin countries in the New World morphing into Candomblé in Brazil, and Santería in Cuba. In Central America, the Aztecs and others combined folk healing with Catholicism as Curanderismo.

These underground traditions from Latin countries blend in the melting pot of the botánica. Among the religious statuary for sale you will find Catholic saints, the Virgin Mary, Native American chiefs, African gods and goddesses, Gypsies, and animals. Lately, you will also find Buddhas and Ganeshas added for good luck. These traditions focused on the building of shrines, so you will find items that would enhance any altar.

Botánicas as urban retail stores carry all kinds of sacred objects for sale: candles, soaps, incense, perfumes, amulets, books, and specialized baths called *limpias* used for purification. You will also find rosary beads and holy water for Roman Catholic practice.

Many Latino immigrants cannot afford and do not trust the American healthcare system. Instead, they rely on the botánica as a place of healing and support. Here they can receive herbal remedies and curative potions, guidance in their personal and spiritual lives, and cures for overcoming evil and bad luck.

In addition to being religious supply stores, alternative healthcare clinics, and spiritual centers, botánicas function for displaced persons from Latino cultures as a connection to one's homeland and its customs. At the botánica they can find hope, healing, support, and spiritual meaning.

The spiritual universe of the botánica is a world of mystery. Mainstream American culture wants everything explained scientifically, and instead, the botánica universe understands that not all can be tied up neatly in a bow. There is a metaphysical appreciation that mystery is a synonym for divinity and spirit. Many of these religions utilize falling into trance states in order to commune with the gods, and some practice animal sacrifice, a practice that goes back hundreds of years to Haitian voodoo and beyond. In fact, in 1993, the U.S. Supreme Court upheld the right of Santería adherents to practice animal sacrifice as part of their religion.

So next time you pass that local botánica in the mini-mall near you ... when you're faced with one of life's inevitable challenges ... maybe a broken heart ... or maybe you need protection from enemies (the two biggest requests) ... maybe, just maybe ... stop in and ask the *curandera* proprietor for help. You may find yourself walking out with not only a red candle for love, or a blue one for peace, but also with a prayer, a hope, a renewed sense that we all live together in a divine universe in which collaboration with Spirit is possible to create our lives.

THE FRUITS & THE NUTS

The type of people attracted to L.A. has always been of a different breed. It began with some of the first white people to hit California: The hundreds of thousands of ambitious young men dreaming to make it rich in the Gold Rush. They left behind in the East and Midwest families, traditions, stability, and values prescribed by an outside authority. These men had stars in their eyes, yes, and that and their independent self-image were traits they shared with the Angelenos of the future.

After the arrival of the railroad in 1882 and the resultant real estate boom, a mythologizing of L.A. and Southern California began to be propagated: "A myth of a very different kind of society – a leisured, elegant life in glorious natural surroundings, a non-competitive society without hierarchy whose people, through the bounty of the land and the generosity of all, were supplied with everything they needed, both physically and spiritually."

The newcomers to L.A. encountered a melting pot of an extremely diverse population unknown back East, which included the Indigenous Peoples, Latinos, Asians, Blacks, and Caucasians. Gays, artists, misfits of all types, and spiritual seekers not wishing to be constrained by traditional, organized religion came here because they knew they would be accepted. This diversity encouraged a live-and-let-live mentality. The myth of California also includes the image of a homogenous group of people who are open, social, future-oriented, working on their human potential and going for the best in life. (Of course, these glowing California myths conveniently ignore the genocide of the Native Peoples, the racial violence, and the fact that millions live in poverty.)

L.A. and California also attracted health seekers who came for the heavenly climate. Many of these were spiritual aspirants unhappy that mainstream religion had abandoned the healing emphasis of Jesus's teachings.

Because the people who moved to L.A. had for the most part left behind traditional values and religion, they were free to develop a spirituality that could be practiced inwardly and alone. Being adventurous in general, they were drawn to alternative worldviews. A certain tolerance and celebration of diversity became guideposts for L.A. spirituality, and remains so today.

In fact, the "original spiritual seekers" may have originated in L.A. In an ad for real estate during the 1880s boom one promoter wrote,

"The vicinity of Los Angeles, the City of the Angels, the site of the very Paradise, ... the graves are actually shown of Adam and Eve, father and mother of man."[*]

In my research for this book, I did not discover the graves of Adam and Eve in L.A., but maybe they are here, hidden, waiting to be discovered by you or one of your friends.

THE SPIRITUAL RENAISSANCE OF THE 20s & 30s

HOLLYWOOD IS A POWERFUL SPIRITUAL VORTEX

"Hollywood" is synonymous with movies, movie stars, fantasy, glitter and bling, and all things superficial and devoid of meaning. However, Hollywood is also a powerful spiritual energy vortex.

The following Spiritual L.A. giants all had their beginnings or arrived and thrived in the early part of the last century and are located within a few mile radius:

- ***Vedanta Temple***
- ***Self-Realization Fellowship***
- ***Church of Scientology***
- ***Monastery of the Angels***
- ***Aetherius Society***
- ***Krotona Institute***
- ***Carroll Righter Foundation (astrology school)***
- ***B.O.T.A.***

And not in Hollywood per se but within a suspiciously close geographical area:

- ***Aimee Semple McPherson and the Angelus Temple***
- ***Bonnie Brae House and the Pentecostal Movement***
- ***PRS***

The founder of the Krotona Institute (see page 60), Albert Powell Warrington, said that he chose its location in Beachwood Canyon (Hollywood Hills) because "not only does the prevailing breeze from the nearby Pacific give physical tone to the surroundings, but a spiritual urge seems to be peculiar to all this section." The hills and groves around Krotona were, it seemed, "magically impregnated."

The energy of the women at the Monastery of the Angels perpetually in prayer and adoration creates a powerful vortex all on its own. And it's not an accident that divine geometry located this place adjacent to the Vedanta Center and all the other spiritual sites listed above.

WHAT ARE VORTEXES?

Anyone who's sensitive cannot deny that certain places carry more spiritual energy than others. Sometimes the energy is high because of the people who've prayed there for decades (or centuries), performed good works there, or perfected themselves to raise their own frequencies. Perhaps a Being of Truth walked there, a Buddha or a Jesus.

Places identified as having high spiritual energy are referred to as energy vortexes. Southern California and L.A. itself are home to quite a few of these whirling hot spots.

Explanations of the what and wherefore of vortexes vary greatly, from the scientific to the most far out. Evidence points to an energy grid similar to the meridians of acupuncture spread over the Earth. At the intersection of these meridians are vortexes where the ancients built famous places of worship: Stonehenge, Machu Picchu, Chichen Itza, many of the cathedrals of Europe, the pyramids of Egypt and the lesser-known pyramids that existed on the banks of the Mississippi River. Today many tourists travel to bask in the vortexes of Sedona and Esalen.

There are reports of increased UFO activity at vortexes, and the appearance of crop circles. Some people believe vortexes to be portals to other dimensions or even the afterlife. Visitors are supposed to be able to tap into their own "higher dimensional selves." People who've spent time at vortexes talk of feelings of well-being, joy, and awe; of having experience of emotional and physical healing or visions; of being filled with spiritual awareness and Universal Consciousness.

From the Joshua Tree Retreat Center's (where there are eighteen reported vortexes) website:

"The energy of a Vortex acts as an amplifier. An amplifier takes a signal or frequency and makes it stronger. When standing in a vortex, the energy will magnify what we bring to it on a physical, mental, emotional or spiritual level. The energy may augment your thoughts and intuition, allowing you to gain an unexpected insight. It may heighten your feelings of joy and happiness or even have physical effect, such as causing a nagging pain to dissipate. The energy may also have a profound spiritual effect, leading a person to gain a greater understanding of who they are, or where they are going in life, many times helping to induce an internal ecstatic experience."

For a list of Ten Southern California Vortexes see page 232.

TOUR

SPIRITUAL L.A. HOLLYWOOD

A spiritual energy vortex for sure – check out this wealth:

1 **Church of Scientology**

The Mothership, the worldwide headquarters, the other Big Blue Whale (see page 40).

4810 Sunset Blvd, Los Angeles, CA 90027

2 **Self-Realization Hollywood Temple**

Tell me it's an accident this is next door to the Church of Scientology ... (see page 44).

4860 Sunset Blvd, Los Angeles, CA 90027

3 **Aetherius Society**

Okay, so they believe Jesus came from Venus ... feel the vibe and let me know (see page 50).

6202 Afton Pl, Los Angeles, CA 90028

4 **Vedanta Temple**

Home to scores of Hollywood and spiritual hipsters, the vibe here is intense (see page 54).

1946 Vedanta Pl, Hollywood, CA 90068-3996

5 **Monastery of Angels**

Ummm... gotta get some of that pumpkin bread (see page 58).

1977 Carmen Ave, Los Angeles, CA 90068

6 **Krotona Apartments**

Very occult, very mysterious ... (see page 60).

2130 Vista Del Mar Ave, Los Angeles, CA 90068

7 **The Source Restaurant**

The site of the former ... (see page 112) (now Cabo Cantina)

8301 Sunset Blvd, West Hollywood, CA 90069

SPIRITUAL L.A. HOLLYWOOD

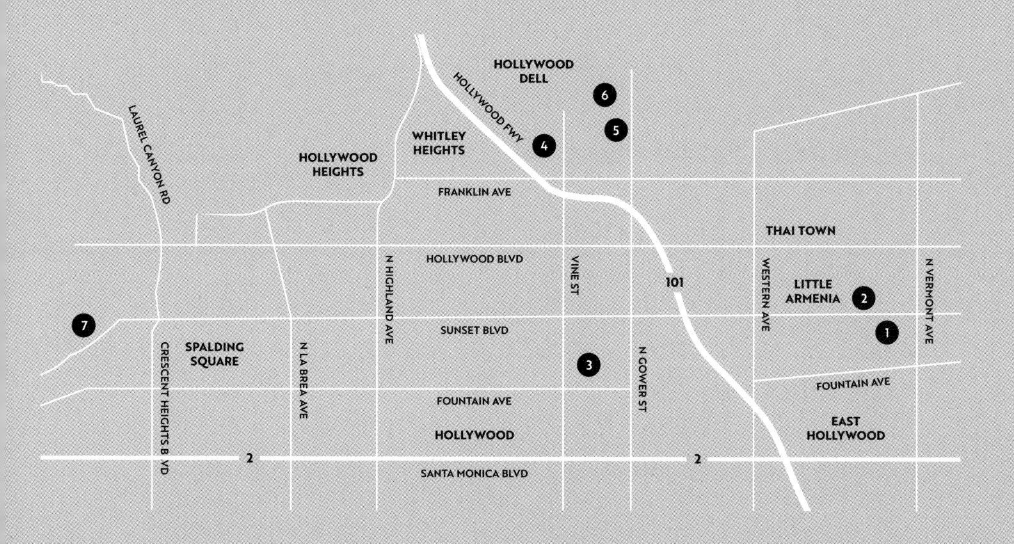

THE BIG SCARY CHURCH THAT ISN'T FRIGHTENING AT ALL (TO VISIT)

To the curious visitor, Scientologists are nothing but friendly and cordial. Of course, we've all heard stories of strange happenings for those who get further involved, but what you'll witness if you visit is normal-looking people spending time and money to improve themselves and their lives.

These are the major L.A. sites:

Church of Scientology of Los Angeles

Scientology's flagship and the center of its worldwide operations is an enormous, blue, former hospital. Visitors are welcome any time they are open, and a friendly staff person will guide you and your friends through the displays and videos. If you want more information it is available; and if not, they will leave you alone unlike the rumors will have you believe. It did seem a little overly-regimented to me until a friend pointed out that the Church receives visitors with ill intentions every single day, so they are correct to protect themselves.
The rooms upstairs are used for people attending trainings. The site includes a full bookstore, is clean and well-lighted, there's free parking and nothing to be afraid of. At least as a visitor.

4810 Sunset Blvd, Los Angeles, CA 90027

Celebrity Centre International

Open to the public, but started for "artists, politicians, leaders of industry, sports figures and anyone with the power and vision to create a better world."
Other Celebrity Centres exist in major cities across the world such as London, Paris, Vienna, and Munich.

5930 Franklin Ave, Los Angeles, CA 90028

Church of Scientology
of Los Angeles

L. Ron Hubbard Life Exhibition

This place is guaranteed to make you wonder "what have I been doing with my life?" as you review L. Ron Hubbard's multitudinous accomplishments: still the youngest boy ever to achieve Eagle Scout, four Guinness World Records: most published author, most translated author, the author with the most audiobook titles and the single most translated non-religious work. His humanitarian efforts, his career as a naval officer, and his wide travels. Whew, and what have you been doing lately?

6331 Hollywood Blvd #100, Los Angeles, CA 90028

Citizens Commission on Human Rights (CCHR) Psychiatry: An Industry of Death Museum

Scientology holds an impassioned and inaccurate belief that psychiatry is evil and up to no good. The displays and videos at this site attempt to prove their position. Personally, I walked out when the introductory video misquoted Freud. While it may be true that psychotropic medications are in some cases over-prescribed, I have seen with my own eyes what a godsend they are for many. Check it out for yourself if interested in an extreme POV.

6616 Sunset Blvd, Los Angeles, CA 90028

WHAT DOES SCIENTOLOGY ACTUALLY TEACH?

It's clear from recent books, films, exposés, and testimonies from former members that the Church of Scientology since David Miscavige took over is abusive and nuts. (Uh oh, am I being monitored?) But what if the writings of L. Ron Hubbard contained some of the most profound spiritual teachings around? What if the situation is similar to that of the relationship between the oftentimes abusive-and-nuts behavior of the Catholic Church and teachings of Jesus?

Okay, L. Ron Hubbard is not Jesus, and I, for the record, am not a Scientologist. But I have looked into it, which I am surprised to find that even the people who consider themselves the most open-minded refuse to do. It's so popular to mindlessly bash Scientology that people miss out on what might be of great benefit to them.

If you want to find out what Scientology actually teaches, search for the Free Zone or Independent Scientologists, people who have left and operate outside the Church. You'll find much of the teachings, which is called The Tech, online for free. It's inspiring and uplifting to read The Tech, which contains principles and axioms for how to effectively act in situations, ideas to actually put into practice in life.

There are helpful diagrams, charts, and scales explaining just about everything.

Some of you have heard of "The Bridge" and "auditing." The Bridge to Total Freedom is a map of higher levels of human development and how to get there, something that mainstream Western psychology has not imagined. People advance up the levels by a process called auditing which clears them of any previous traumas and unhelpful beliefs.

Scientology's moral code is "The greatest good for the greatest number." They don't believe in original sin, rather in the innate goodness of human beings. People are seen as immortal beings having multiple lifetimes during which time we evolve. There is a popular program called the Purification Rundown, which is a detox program to clear the body of all toxins and drugs.

Part of how Scientology has gotten into trouble is by its handling of "justice," that is, its approval of smashing one's enemies or those who counter Scientology in any way.
This leads to "disconnecting" with anyone who disagrees, something common to cult behavior.

Anyway, check it out for yourself. Even if you don't agree with what you read, it's guaranteed you'll find it fascinating.

YOGANANDA AND THE WEST'S FIRST VIEW OF THE EAST

Levitating saints, a swami materializing a palace in the Himalayas, the woman yogi who never eats: these are just a few of the wonders encountered by over four million readers of Paramahansa Yogananda's *Autobiography of a Yogi*. The book has served many seekers as their first introduction to Eastern spirituality, including Steve Jobs who said he first read it as a teen and once a year thereafter.

Yogananda arrived in the U.S. from India in 1920, embarking on a cross-county speaking tour that attracted thousands everywhere he went. In 1925, he landed in L.A. and stayed, establishing an international spiritual empire which in L.A. includes the headquarters of his organization, the Self Realization Fellowship (SRF), the Hollywood Temple, his burial place at Forest Lawn, and the Lake Shrine.

Yogananda was the first to widely introduce yoga, meditation, and the idea that a universal Truth underlies all religions. He and his acolytes teach *kriya yoga*, a breath technique that can only be passed on by an initiated guru. Yogananda was a prolific author and lecturer, and was well loved by many then and now. He died in 1952 in downtown L.A. at the Biltmore Hotel after finishing a lecture.

One of the most amazing miracles of Yogananda's story is that there is documented evidence that his body did not decay for at least the twenty days before it was interred. At the end of *Autobiography*, you can read the notarized letter by the mortuary director attesting to "the absence of any visual signs of decay in the dead body of Paramahansa Yogananda offers the most extraordinary case in our experience ... Yogananda's body was apparently in a phenomenal state of immutability."

When Yogananda left Daya Mata as his successor, it was new for an Indian guru to pass leadership to a woman. The organization split in 1960 when Kriyananda (born Donald Walters) was kicked out of SRF and founded his own organization, Ananda, which also has active centers in L.A. and all over the world. Since 2014, another female direct disciple of Yogananda, Mrinalini Mata, has been in charge.

Yogananda and his teachings came to popular attention with the 2014 release of the film *Awake: The Life of Yogananda*. This compelling documentary traces Yogananda's life from a young man in India to his stature as one of the teachers most responsible for bringing the wisdom of the East to the West.

If you consider yourself spiritual but not religious, chances are you owe a debt to the life and work of Paramahansa Yogananda.

Photos left + right: Yogananda headquarters

L.A. YOGANANDA EMPIRE

Paramahansa Yogananda's reach was immeasurable, elevating the consciousness of millions worldwide; and we are lucky here in L.A. to be able to visit sacred spots where he actually walked and taught. To see and feel the energy of these places quiets the mind and helps one center on what's really important.

All of the Self Realization Fellowship (SRF) locations have beautifully landscaped meditation gardens, quiet, peaceful atmospheres, tempting gift stores, and friendly staff waiting to answer all your questions.

1 International Headquarters, Self-Realization Fellowship (also known as the Mount Washington Center)

Back in the day Yogananda himself could often be seen sweeping the front porch of the administration building, a former hotel. Inside are offices, a chapel, and a library with artifacts of Yogananda's life such as handwritten letters, and one of his tunics. The energy emanating from them is powerful if you tune in. Behind the building you'll find a charming wooden bridge and a pond full of mouth-open, hungry koi fish.

The grounds invite meditation with secluded nooks spread all around. Look for the Temple of Leaves – a circular line of benches under a canopy of trees. Many claim to have had an overpowering energy experience while meditating there. Three separate staffers told me to not miss a visit to the wishing well because, "all wishes made here will come true." I wished really hard, and mine came true – just not the way I'd hoped. Maybe yours will.

3880 San Rafael Ave, Los Angeles, CA 90065

2 Hollywood Temple, Self-Realization Fellowship

Smack in the center of Hollywood, next door to the behemoth Scientology mothership, is the oldest of the SRF's American churches founded by Yogananda. The staff is happy to offer an impromptu tour, and the one I took included visitors from Australia and Botswana. The temple is noted for its stained-glass windows, and there is a special Children's Garden with mosaics and stone rabbits. Most people would never guess that that such a lovely meditation oasis lies in the heart of bustling Hollywood.

Be sure to snap a photo of the street sign of the alley named Ashram Drive. Free Parking: the entrance is on the east side of Edgemont St., about fifty feet south of Sunset Blvd.

4860 W Sunset Blvd, Hollywood, CA 90027

3 Burial Place of Yogananda Forest Lawn Memorial Park

Forest Lawn cemetery is known for its flamboyant style and as the final resting place of numerous movie stars from the Golden Age of Hollywood, such as Clark Gable, Jean Harlow, and Humphrey Bogart. Michael Jackson is buried there though not in a location open to the public.

The guard at the front gate will happily direct you to Yogananda's burial site. Park in front of the mausoleum, and enter the narrow passageway on the left. Ring the buzzer, and tell them you are here to visit Yogananda. Once inside you will be amazed at the sight of the lofty vaulted ceilings and long hallways, the cold refrigerated air. Turn right

L.A. YOGANANDA EMPIRE

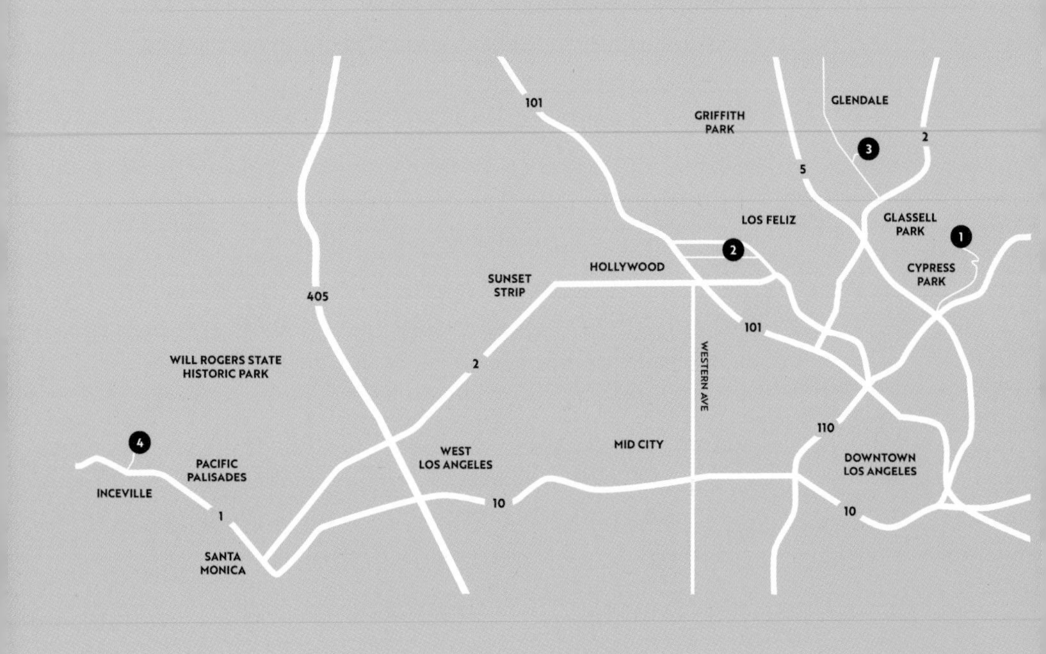

where the chain has been taken down: that is where Yogananda's body resides, always accompanied by fresh flowers left by devotees.

Some say that because of the level of awareness Yogananda achieved before he died, his consciousness is alive inside the crypt. Whether or not this is true, being in his presence inspires great feelings of reverence and a quiet mind. It always brings me to my knees, bowing as we did in India before great saints. The energy of this powerful Master is palpable, one of the most powerful outpourings of shakti in our fair City of the Angels.

1712 S Glendale Ave, Glendale, CA 91205

4 The Lake Shrine

The Lake Shrine is a sheer delight: meditative and calm, steeped in spiritual history and vibe, yet universally beautiful enough to bring your non-spiritual family and friends. Right up the hill from the Pacific Coast Highway, the ten-acre grounds are designed for a leisurely stroll around the lake. Some of the highlights on your path: ducks and swans, a shrine with a portion of Gandhi's ashes, a windmill, an old boat, a chapel, little plaques with sayings from different religions, a gift store I can never resist, a museum, and quiet spots for meditation. A visit to the Lake Shrine is always calming and balancing whether you stay for a quick stroll or sit all day.

Self-Realization Fellowship Lake Shrine
17190 Sunset Blvd, Pacific Palisades, CA 90272

To complete your Southland Tour of the Yogananda Empire, take a day trip down to Encinitas: (See page 217)

SRF Lake Shrine

The Aetherius Society American Headquarters

JESUS CAME FROM OUTER SPACE

It would be easy to make fun of the Aetherius Society if one were so inclined. This international spiritual organization is "dedicated to spreading and acting upon the teachings of advanced extraterrestrials." Its motto is "Co-operating with Gods from Space."

But are you so inclined to mock when you learn that the most important teaching of the Aetherians is selfless service to others? That they accept and honor every other religion's beliefs and promote compassion and working for a better world?

The American Headquarters of the Aetherius Society is located on a quiet, residential, garden-like street in Hollywood. Sharing leadership with the headquarters in London, they have outposts in eleven countries with membership numbering in the thousands.

The founder, Dr. George King, lived in L.A. and developed the Society and its mission from the mid-1950s until his death in 1997. Previously, King had been practicing yoga for eight to ten hours a day when he said he was contacted by an ET named Aetherius hailing from Venus, which is where Buddha and Jesus also reside. Dr. King continued to communicate with ET's for over forty years and taught that ET's are compassionate and here to help us create a better world.

The Society shares the belief of many of the newer religions especially Theosophy: that there is One Truth in many forms, the power of prayer, yoga, and kundalini, the laws of karma, the presence of Ascended Masters, and that spiritual and psychic powers are available for anyone to develop. In fact, Dr. King highly recommended reading *Autobiography of a Yogi*.

Another cool thing they believe is that mountains are holy and hence lead monthly pilgrimages to Mount Baldy from May to October. A yearly World Peace Pilgrimage is celebrated on Mount Baldy in cooperation with other religions. Check it out on their website.

It all seemed strange to me at first, I must admit; but when I visited everybody appeared completely normal. Pat, who answered all our questions, looked and acted like a retired schoolteacher. The sincerity of the Aetherians and their desire to be of service is undeniable. Anyone working to promote more compassion in the world has my vote.

The Aetherius Society American Headquarters

6202 Afton Pl, Los Angeles, CA 90028

UFO ACTIVITY IN GREATER L.A.

Are UFOs and aliens spiritual beings? Do they belong in a book about L.A. Spirituality? Plenty of people in the Southland believe they are and do. More Angelenos than you might imagine claim to have interacted with entities from other planets who amazed, instructed, and enlightened them.

Three areas in Greater L.A. report heightened UFO activity: Topanga Canyon and the Santa Monica Mountains, the desert around Joshua Tree, and Catalina Island.

In the early 1990s in Topanga, a gigantic wave of hundreds of UFO sightings occurred, all reported by a cross section of reputable people. The area has been designated a "flap area" since 1947, that is, an area with a disproportionate number of UFO reports. People described experiencing strange lights, ships, missing time periods, and actual encounters with and abductions by aliens.

The 1950s saw a flurry of activity in the desert around Joshua Tree with the sightings at Giant Rock (see page 180) and the building of the Integratron (see page 176) reportedly at the direction of aliens. The Interplanetary Spacecraft Convention was held annually from 1954-1978 at Giant Rock with thousands of attendees.

Depending on whom you talk with, and the locals are quite adamant, UFO sightings remain common to this day.

There have been hundreds of sightings on Catalina Island, enough to support a tour according to its website, but the "tour" is non-responsive.

Worldwide it is reported that UFOs are most often sighted in rural regions containing mountains and valleys that are close to cities. These flap areas are often near military bases, and there is frequently the strong presence of Native American culture both past and present. UFOs seem attracted to areas with powerful energy vortexes. (see page 232) All of these characteristics match the descriptions of Topanga Canyon, Joshua Tree, and Catalina Island.

See also the Aetherius Society (see page 50) for people who worship alien beings.

ALDOUS WAS HERE

The first time I visited the Hollywood Vedanta Temple, I nearly passed out from the spiritual energy there. I had wanted to check it out because of its affiliation with the glamorous group of writers and mystics who gathered around Aldous and Laura Huxley (see page 56), and because I had read in *The Knee of Listening*, that its author, Adi Da Samraj, had achieved enlightenment in the Temple. I suspected there might be powerful energy there.

I was not disappointed. As soon as I entered the Temple, bowed at the altar, and took my seat, I promptly fell into a deep meditative state. Only when I looked at my watch did I realize I had been "out" for two and a half hours. As monk Jnana Chaitanya stated, "Some very holy people lived and taught here and contributed a great deal to the vibration."

Vedanta is an ancient Hindu religion whose main teaching is the oneness of all, respect for all including all religions, and that God dwells within all hearts. The main teachers were Swami Ramakrishna and Sri Sarada Devi ("Holy Mother") who were a married couple, and later, Swami Vivekananda. The religion emphasizes the journey to the discovery of God within and the mystic path. The main headquarters is in India.

The Vedanta Temple is located in the midst of a quiet residential community right by the Hollywood Freeway. Built in 1938, it has the onion-domed temple with padded pews inside, the bookstore, offices, and a monastery where eighteen swamis and eighteen nuns reside.

The bookstore is quite a treasure, carrying books from all traditions. I have to warn you, however, they turned down my book, *Shortcuts to Mindfulness* as being "too alternative."

Hollywood Vedanta Temple

1946 Vedanta Pl, Hollywood, CA 90068-3996

Photo right:
Hollywood Vedanta Temple

THE HUXLEYS IN PARADISE

Most everyone knows The Doors as one of the, if not the, quintessential L.A. bands. Perhaps only rock aficionados know that The Doors took their name from Aldous Huxley's book *The Doors of Perception*, a chronicle of his experiences exploring mescaline. This British-born author, most widely known for *Brave New World*, a sci-fi novel in which the world's inhabitants lie around hypnotized by legal drugs and entertainment (sound familiar?), was experimenting with spirituality and mind-expansion here in L.A. from 1937 until his death in 1963, which he chose to undergo while taking LSD.

Aldous Huxley (1894–1963) was admired worldwide for his intellect and fearless investigations into life. His work was nominated seven times for the Nobel Prize in Literature. He was a novelist, essayist, and social critic who also wrote screenplays for Hollywood. As a scholar of mysticism, he wrote *The Perennial Philosophy*, a seminal book about the deep universal Truth underlying all religions.

More interesting, perhaps, was his hipster life: Huxley lived surrounded by the artists and intelligentsia of his day: D.H. Lawrence, the Bloomsbury group, Igor Stravinsky, Greta Garbo, Charlie Chaplin, Christopher Isherwood, Ram Das and Timothy Leary. Glamorous and handsome, Huxley always wore dapper suits and was rumored to have had an "interesting" sex life.

It was in L.A. that Huxley's search took a serious turn toward the spiritual. He became a dedicated student of Eastern philosophy, frequenting the Vedanta Temple in Hollywood. (see page 54). Huxley studied yoga with Krishnamurti and practiced meditation and vegetarianism.

It was also in L.A. that he married his second wife, Laura Huxley, who went on to become a prominent psychotherapist and quite the scenester herself. Laura authored five books, the most famous being *You are Not the Target*. Long after Aldous' death, she was always on the guest list of the most desirable gatherings in town, most often to be seen with her trademark white hat tipped saucily over one eye.

Aldous Huxley used to hang out at the Farmer's Market
3rd and Fairfax.

And lived at the following addresses:

- *1340 N Laurel Ave, West Hollywood, CA 90046 (1938)*
- *1320 N Crescent Heights Blvd, Hollywood, CA 90046 (1939)*
- *701 S Amalfi Dr, Pacific Palisades, CA 90272 (1939-42)*
- *145 ½ Doheny Dr, Los Angeles, CA 90048 (1943)*
- *740 N Kings Rd, Los Angeles, CA 90069 (1949)*

And lived with Laura and took his final dose of LSD at

- *6233 Mulholland Hwy, Los Angeles, CA 90068*

THE PUMPKIN BREAD NUNS

"I think that's the monastery Katy Perry is buying," Russ said as he pulled the flat iron through my hair. (Russ Hart is a genius hairstylist and can be contacted at LaBonté Hart Salon.)

I quickly Googled to find out that yes, Katy Perry was fighting developers to buy her own monastery, and yes, the nuns were being "relocated." I decided I'd better head down ASAP in case closure was imminent, and I forever missed tasting their famous pumpkin bread.

The Monastery of the Angels was established in Hollywood in 1934 by nuns with a lineage stretching back to 1207. Sixteen cloistered sisters live within: they pray; they work, worship, study, and at times observe silence; never coming out to mix with the rest of us. The sisters partially support their mission by making and selling pumpkin bread which is available for purchase in the gift shop along with rosaries and other religious artifacts.

These nuns at the Monastery of the Angels are special because they have been given permission to perform the Perpetual Adoration of the Blessed Sacrament, meaning that 24/7, one of them is kneeling before the altar and praying for us and for the salvation of the world. That much prayer going on anywhere sets up a purifying, sanctified energy field, building a strong spiritual vortex that affects everyone in L.A. whether they know it or not.

At a party on the Westside a few nights after my visit, I chatted with Matt, a tall, handsome spiritual hipster well known among the kirtan community. We've been to some of the same places in India, and we once hung out and ate *idlis* together. I told him about my visit to the Monastery and about the Perpetual Adoration.

"That's creepy," he said.
"Creepy?" I asked, quite taken aback. "They're praying for us 24/7."
"Yeah," he said, "but what are they praying for? Nuns? It's creepy."

The Monastery of the Angels

You know, if it were sexless Tibetan monks chanting *om mani padme hum* 24/7, Matt and everyone else would consider that the coolest thing on earth. But since these are celibate women, and even worse, Christian, it is apparently not in the realm of New Age trendy. I realize that nuns and organized religion are out of favor today, but really, the fact that these women are on their knees forever and always praying for our betterment, for this we could choose to be grateful.

By the way, the pumpkin bread tastes just like Grandma used to make. And for the record, Katy Perry is buying a DIFFERENT monastery. How L.A. is that?

The Monastery of the Angels

1977 Carmen Ave, Los Angeles, CA 90068

KROTONA
OF OLD HOLLYWOOD
EST. 1912
APARTMENTS 323.465.3595

THE SECRETS OF KROTONA

Today it's an almost-tacky, run-down, run-of-the-mill apartment building in the Hollywood Hills, Beachwood Canyon to be exact. But in its heyday, the Krotona Apartments were a hotbed of occult activity hosting a temple, a metaphysical library, a vegetarian cafeteria, a theater, a "magnetically charged" meditation room, and a fascinating cast of characters such as Charlie Chaplin and Annie Besant. It was the headquarters of the Esoteric School, the Temple of the Rosy Cross, and the Order of the Eastern Star.

Begun by the Theosophical Society (see page 63) in 1912, the Krotona community consisted of eleven acres in Beachwood Canyon hosting homes for about five hundred people. The seventeen-unit Krotona Apartments were its center. The complex was to be an institute of higher learning and research on the subtler aspects of science including psychology and psychic phenomena. After all, the Theosophical Society's mission was to "explore the inexplicable."

In 1926 the community relocated to Ojai (see page 208) citing the growing influence of urban Hollywood. The Krotona Apartments have continued to be populated by artists, hipsters, and spiritual explorers ever since. In the 60s and 70s there were reported LSD parties around the courtyard's lotus pond, and guitar sessions with the likes of members of Jimi Hendrix's band. It is rumored that Quentin Tarantino crashed on the couch of a screenwriter resident for seven months. Plus, the hundreds of intriguing characters whose names we will never know.

Photos left + right:
Krotona Apartments

Krotona courtyard lotus pond

If you visit, you can still see the lotus pond resting quietly in the center court, keeping any previous occult or bohemian activity a secret. Upstairs you'll find a building with a Moorish-style dome and a circular stained-glass window. That symbol is a Rosicrucian seal, and the door is to the former Grand Temple of the Holy Cross. Very little other information offers itself, and the mind wanders to fantasies of what may have gone on inside these walls. Or what's going on inside them today, for that matter.

Krotona Apartments

2130 Vista Del Mar Ave, Los Angeles, CA 90068

THE THEOSOPHICAL SOCIETY AND BAD-ROCKSTAR BEHAVIOR

If you were interested enough to pick up this book, you've undoubtedly been influenced by the Theosophical Society (TS) whether you know it or not. The TS has been a major conduit for Eastern thought into the West, and is thus a progenitor of alternative spirituality and the New Age movement. The main beliefs include karma, reincarnation, the essential Oneness of all, and that there is a perennial philosophy underlying the world religions.

The Theosophical Society was begun in New York City in 1875. One of its founders was Helena Petrovna Blavatsky (1831 – 1891), the Russian occultist, author, philosopher, world traveler, and one of the most flamboyant spiritual rockstars of all time. Even her biographers don't believe all the tales she told, as she deliberately falsified and glamorized her past.

However, much of it was true, and it is a wonderful saga: Madame Blavatsky began traveling the world in search of esoteric knowledge while still quite young, and claimed she met a group of adepts, the Masters of Ancient Wisdom, who communicated with her telepathically and directed her to go to Tibet to develop her psychic powers. She wrote two highly influential books, *Isis Unveiled* and *The Secret*

Doctrine: The Synthesis of Science, Religion, and Philosophy, gaining an international following. Madame was highly charismatic, had incredible energy and a terrible temper, swore profusely, was obese, chain-smoked, and had "utter disregard for the Victorian code of morality." Helena Blavatsky lived by no rules other than her own.

Rumors (some of which she propagated) circulated concerning her exploits include many signs of bad-rockstar behavior: public accusations that she produced fake paranormal phenomena, that she contacted spirits of the dead, that she saved an opera singer from being murdered, that she survived a shipwreck, that she studied with First Nations people in Quebec, that she was a Russian spy. It is a known fact that Blavatsky was a bigamist, that is, married to two men at the same time, and that one of her husbands sued for divorce when she refused to consummate the marriage. She lived in a celibate relationship with Colonel Olcott, another founder of the TS, in an apartment in New York called the Lamasery which was decorated with spiritual figures and taxidermied animals. There they gave lectures and held séances.

The TS was involved in the World Teacher Project from the 1880s to 1929. The TS had felt it was the right time for an appearance of a World Teacher, and when they discovered the fourteen-year old Jiddu Krishnamurti (see page 210) proclaimed him the One. He was taken in, extensively taught esoteric secrets and groomed for the role. In 1929 when he was to be presented to the world, much to the dismay of the TS, Krishnamurti took the stage and announced that he was not the World Teacher. He subsequently left the TS and went on to teach his own version of spirituality.

The organization Blavatsky helped create, the TS, became internationally known, influencing people as reputable as Gandhi and Thomas Edison, and still exists today. There are over one hundred and twenty-one lodges of the group charted around the world. The Theosophical Society is visible in L.A. history in the Krotona movement (see page 60), Manly P. Hall and PRS (see page 66), Krishnamurti, and its local chapters, and its themes run through New Thought and others.

The International Headquarters of the TS is in Pasadena, although there is no physical location, only a PO box.

The United Lodge of Theosophists (ULT), one of the four main branches of the original movement, offers a full schedule of free classes and workshops.

Theosophy Hall

245 W 33rd St, Los Angeles, CA 90007

WANT TO LEARN THE SECRET TEACHINGS OF ALL AGES?

Few of the daily commuters passing the PRS building on Los Feliz Boulevard have ever imagined that it holds one of the world's foremost occult libraries with over fifty thousand books. There are so many books on spirituality, religion, and metaphysics that there are even rumored to be secret black magic texts only available with the librarian's permission.

The Philosophical Research Society (PRS) was founded in 1934 by Manly P. Hall (1901 - 1990). Hall was one of the first writers to make occult teachings available to the mainstream in his book *The Secret Teachings of All Ages*. *Secret Teachings* is often considered the most beautiful and complete book on the occult ever written, and it is written in brief chapters that are easily digested in a short sitting.

The building also contains the University of Philosophical Research. UPR teaches the world's wisdom traditions. The school offers three nationally accredited online degree programs (M.A. in Consciousness Studies, M.A. in Transformational Psychology, and Bachelor of Arts program in Liberal Studies).

Unlike the University of Santa Monica, which is a shill organization for the teachings of John-Roger and MSIA, The University of P.R. is based on the premise of inclusion of all traditions and beliefs, and for the students to decide what they believe for themselves.

The Philosophical Research Society and the University of Philosophical Research
3910 Los Feliz Blvd, Los Angeles, CA 90027

Photos left + right:
University of Philosophical Research

THE PARSONAGE OF
AIMEE SEMPLE MCPHERSO
The Parsonage of
Aimee Semple McPherson
Mondays – Thursdays 1 – 3 PM
Fridays 10 – 1 PM
(213) 989-4444

SHE WAS SEXY; SHE WAS HOT, AND SHE SERVED GOD

Aimee Semple McPherson's (1890- 1944) charisma was legendary, her theatrical sense: genius. Arriving in L.A. in 1918 with one hundred dollars, an old beat-up car, and two children, by 1925 she had built an international empire worth more than a million dollars with property of $250,000. (Those numbers are impressive today, but imagine what they would be calculated for inflation.) At the height of her fame, her Angelus Temple was filled with five thousand worshippers three services a day, seven days a week, listening to her preach the word of God and watching the best show in town, which once included her chasing the devil around the stage with a pitchfork.

Although she was the first woman to start her own denomination, the Foursquare Church, of which there are today sixteen hundred churches with a membership of eight million worldwide, it is her risqué personal life for which she is most remembered. Married three times, she was involved in a scandal from which her reputation never recovered.

Photo left: The Parsonage of Aimee Semple McPherson

In 1926, Sister Aimee, wearing a bathing suit, walked into the water off Ocean Park and disappeared. Thousands flocked to the beach to pray for her return, and a plane dropped flowers onto the ocean where she had been "lost." The Church raised $35,000 in her memory. However, Aimee was later located in Agua Prieta, Mexico, where it was claimed she had escaped with her lover and former employee, Kenneth Ormiston. When Aimee returned to L.A., it was the return of a Queen: she exited the train onto a carpet of roses, and a band played as she paraded down the street with an escort of twenty cowboys and police squads.

She was arrested but the charges were never proven and were dropped. What crime had she committed, after all? Perhaps Sister Aimee's success was a thorn in the side of the Protestant clergy, and this trial and harassment had been merely a way to try to besmirch her reputation and popularity.

The Angelus Temple

Despite the scandal and showmanship, Aimee Semple McPherson certainly was a dedicated server of the spiritual. She preached her Foursquare Gospel that taught salvation, the Second Coming, the possibility of redemption, and physical healing through prayer. She herself never claimed to be able to heal the sick, but her fans said otherwise. During her lifetime she prayed for the healing of three hundred thousand people, and her ministries fed over a million people during the Depression.

Her funeral in 1944 at Forest Lawn was the biggest L.A. had yet seen. Her death was ruled an accidental overdose of barbiturates, rather than, as some said, a suicide. Her son, Rolf, continued her work for the next forty-four years.

The Angelus Temple

Now a National Historic Landmark, Sister Aimee dedicated this church in 1925, and from here administered her empire. Today it is a Latino Pentecostal church preaching the gospel, offering schools and camps for children, and actively providing programs that feed the poor and sponsor refugees. Great to take a walk around Echo Park Lake, admire the Temple, and imagine how it must have been in its glory days.

1100 Glendale Blvd, Los Angeles, CA 90026

The Parsonage of Aimee Semple McPherson

Next door to the Angelus Temple is a supercool museum of Sister Aimee's life including photos, personal artifacts, and displays of her theatrical costumes.

1801 Park Ave, Los Angeles, CA 90026

WHOLE LOTTA SHAKIN'

The Pentecostal movement -- the Christian sect including speaking in tongues, baptism in the Holy Spirit, charismatic preachers, healings -- that must have started in the Deep South, right? Actually, it started right here in L.A. in Echo Park.

William J. Seymour, a Black, one-eyed preacher who was the son of slaves, had come out from the Midwest and built a small but avid following at the home of Richard and Ruth Asberry at what is now called the Bonnie Brae House. On April 9, 1906, when this group of African-Americans had gathered to fast and pray to receive the holy spirit, one of them, Edward S. Lee, began speaking in tongues, and six others followed. It was an ecstatic moment of outpouring of Divine energy, and the intensity blossomed and swelled. It filled up the house, and poured down the street, and entered the hearts and spirits of willing Angelenos.

It spread out so far that within three days the House and the surrounding streets were jam-packed with crowds of all income levels and ethnicities – Blacks, Caucasians, and Latinos -- speaking in tongues, singing, and shouting. People reported being knocked to the ground by the power of spirit. Cries of joy could be heard throughout the neighborhood. The worshipping went on continually night and day until finally, the front porch of the house started shaking and collapsed from the rapturous celebration.

Seymour's preaching must have been phenomenal, because the word is still spreading. You can imagine how high the energy must have been – utterly joyful, ecstatic, blissed out. A bit of that vortex power remains – can you feel it?

Bonnie Brae House

Bonnie Brae House

Tours are available at the Bonnie Brae House, and even overnight stays. If interested, call ahead. On the other hand, when we went to view the house on our own, a neighbor came up and told us the inside story and more. Maybe you'll be so lucky.

📍 ***214 N Bonnie Brae St, Los Angeles, CA 90026***

Azusa Street Revival

The congregation moved to a location on Azusa Street, growing to fifteen hundred people attending a day. Services went on 24/7, and thousands and thousands of people were baptized in the Holy Spirit. Azusa Street is considered the birthplace of the Pentecostal movement by most everyone. By 1913, the enthusiasm had waned at Azusa Street, but Pentecostalism spread rapidly around the globe and is today the fastest-growing religion in the world, second only to Roman Catholicism, numbering over six hundred million believers.

📍 ***312 Azusa St, Los Angeles, CA 90012***
(now part of the Japanese-American Cultural and Community Center)

THE MOUNT HELIOS LOVE CULT

The neighbors found Edith suspicious on account of her hair being "bobbed in true radical style." They fussed about "weird proceedings reported to be of lurid character." The misfits over there on Mount Helios flew a "crimson love flag," and participated in "revels and weird rituals." Further evidence of dubious activity was that red light that kept burning in the window overnight.

Edith Maida Lessing (born TX 1875- died 1939 in L.A.) was an accomplished composer, lyricist, songwriter, and poet. Two of her popular songs were "Just as the Ship went Down" and "Oh! You Circus Day." Books of her poems and sheet music are still available on Amazon today and you can hear one of her songs performed on YouTube.

Ms. Lessing was also the founder and leader of the Mount Helios "love cult" which flourished in the early 1920s atop a hill in Glassell Park, a neighborhood of Northeast L.A. Edith's radical views included her belief that free love would replace marriage, and the rightness of the communal ownership of property. At Mount Helios, people lived in tents and shacks, with Edith presiding dressed in a purple gown trimmed with gold. Edith proclaimed that she had control over a thousand men, although what kind of control she meant (sexual?) we don't know.

Edith Maida Lessing's final resting place at Forest Lawn

According to a report in the *Los Angeles Herald*, in 1921 police began investigating "the extent of her radical beliefs." Another suspicious neighbor testified that Mount Helios had presented a play in which "the men wore loin cloths and the women only thin draperies." In 1922, Edith Maida Lessing was found guilty of criminal syndication for sending "obscene" material through the mail. She was sentenced to two years in the Reformatory for Women in Missouri. Thus, the Mount Helios experiment in radical living was effectively brought down and ended.

Buried at Forest Lawn Memorial Park Glendale

Sunrise Slope, Map 1, Lot 5788, space 2
(There's no marker. What a shame.)

THE LIZARD PEOPLE WHO LIVED UNDER L.A.

Hopi Indian legend told of Snake Brothers who built and occupied underground cities in what are now California, Arizona, Mexico and Central America. These people and settlements were believed to have vanished five thousand years ago.

In 1934, an article was published in the *Los Angeles Times* that one of the Hopi lost cities was believed to be underneath downtown L.A. This settlement was believed to be in the shape of a lizard: the head at Dodger Stadium and the tail beneath the Central Library. Warren Shufelt, a mining engineer, was so sure the remains of this lost city would be found that he was ready to dig up the downtown financial district. His research was actually authorized by the city council, but later dropped.

The subterranean city was believed to house not only thousands of families, but also golden tablets with occult knowledge of the origin of humanity.

Shufelt never found the Lizard City despite his extensive mapping. Mysterious tunnels have been unearthed in downtown L.A., but they've usually been seen as the work of smugglers and other ne'er-do-wells.

OCCULT L.A. & THE WESTERN TRADITION

TOUR

EASTSIDE SPIRITUAL L.A.

L.A.'s Eastside is full of mystical and spiritual treasure:

1 International Headquarters, Self-Realization Fellowship (also known as the Mount Washington Center)

Yogananda himself used to sweep the porch here (see page 46).

3880 San Rafael Ave, Los Angeles, CA 90065

2 Angelus Temple

Sister Aimee's masterpiece (see page 69).

1100 Glendale Blvd, Los Angeles, CA 90026

Photo left: Peace Awareness Labyrinth & Gardens

3 **The Parsonage of Aimee Semple McPherson**

Supercool museum of Sister Aimee's life.

1801 Park Ave, Los Angeles, CA 90026

4 **Philosophical Research Society**

Secrets galore housed in the library of over fifty thousand books (see page 66).

3910 Los Feliz Blvd, Los Angeles, CA 90027

5 **Bonnie Brae House**

All that shakin' and rockin' and rollin' – can you feel it? (see page 72)

214 N Bonnie Brae St, Los Angeles, CA 90026

Mark Phillips and Martin Anguiano
Spellbound Sky

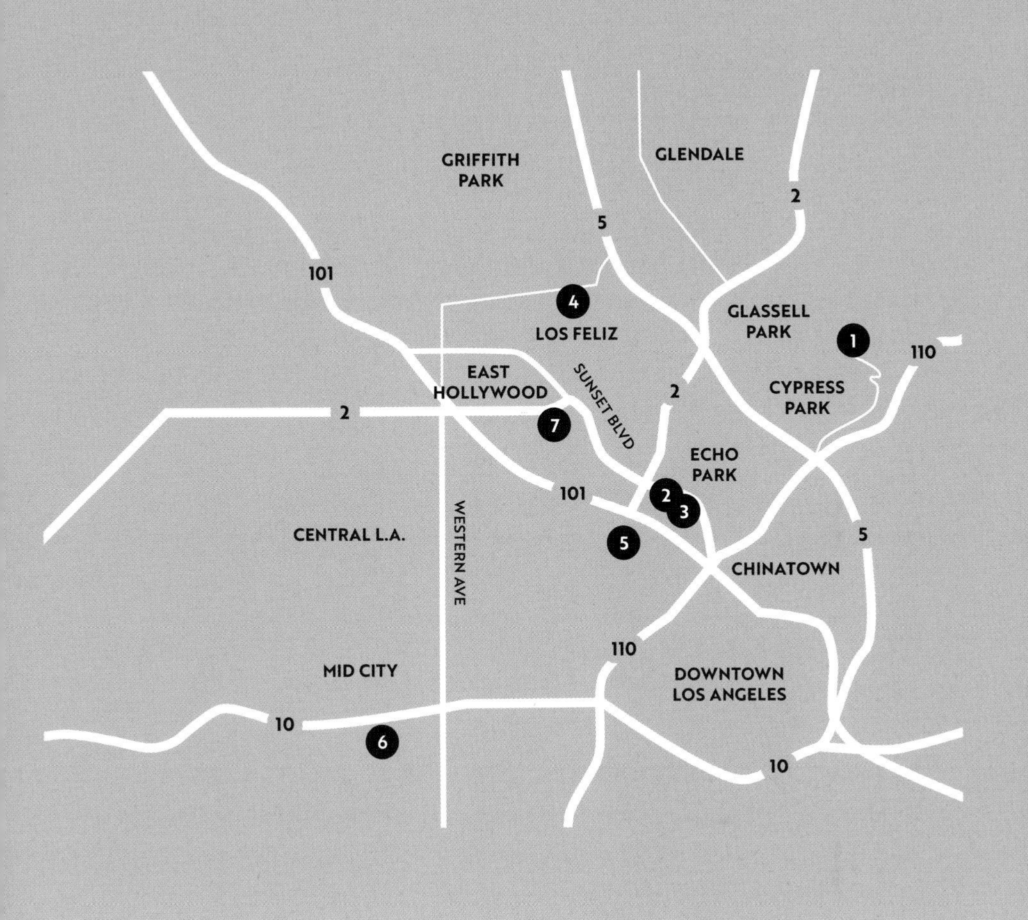

6 Peace Awareness Labyrinth & Gardens

Urban meditation oasis. Entrance is free but you must call ahead: (323) 737-4055

3500 W Adams Blvd, Los Angeles, CA 90018

7 Spellbound Sky

Go just to meet Mark and Martin. Pick up a crystal while you're there (see page 227).

4210 Santa Monica Blvd, Los Angeles, CA 90029

NINE FAMOUS AND INFAMOUS LOS ANGELES OCCULTISTS

One would expect L.A. to have over-the-top and charismatic occult celebrities, and these characters who also took prominence on the world stage do not disappoint. All have fascinating biographies that would be worth your while to explore further:

Kenneth Anger (1927-present) Most well-known for his popular celebrity exposés *Hollywood Babylon I and II*, Anger is an openly gay underground filmmaker who has produced close to forty works. A devotee of Aleister Crowley (see page 86), the films *Inauguration of the Pleasure Dome* (starring Marjorie Cameron) and *Scorpio Rising* (1964) deal with occult themes. "Of course," Anger is quoted as saying, "My definition of evil is not everybody else's."

Marjorie Cameron (1922-1995) A serious occult practitioner, Cameron and her husband, Jack Parsons, were students of Aleister Crowley and performed magickal rituals meant to herald in a new age. A retrospective of her work, *Cameron: Songs for the Witch Woman* was held in 2014 at the Museum of Contemporary Art, Los Angeles (MOCA) which finally gave Marjorie Cameron her due as an important figure in the history of L.A. art.

Paul Foster Case (1884-1954) The author of numerous books on the occult who founded the Builders of the Adytum (B.O.T.A.). Still headquartered in L.A. today, B.O.T.A. is a correspondence school covering practically all of the Western mystery tradition: tarot, Kabbalah, metaphysics, magic, and alchemy.

Manly P. Hall (1901-1990) Best known for his book, *The Secret Teachings of All Ages* (1928), Hall founded the Philosophical Research Society (PRS) in Los Angeles. He wrote over 150 books and essays and gave approximately eight thousand lectures on the occult in the US and abroad.

Sybil Leek (1917–1982) wrote *Diary of a Witch* (1968) and over sixty other books that brought Wicca and the metaphysical arts to the mainstream. The BBC named her "Britain's most famous witch" before she moved to L.A. due to, she said, "too many people visiting me to see what a witch looks like." She appeared on many TV and radio programs including the popular 60s show, *To Tell the Truth.*

Maja D'Aoust, the White Witch (1974-present) Popular today, written about in *L.A. Weekly* and *L.A. Magazine*, Maja is a full-time occultist who has studied widely and earned her M.A. in transformational psychology. She leads tours, lectures, and gives readings based on astrology, Jung, and ancient Greek and Hermetic philosophies.

Jack Parsons (1914-1952) Finally, a real "rocket scientist" who was one of the principal founders of the Jet Propulsion Laboratory (JPL) in Pasadena as well as associated with the California Institute of Technology (Caltech). Along with his wife, Marjorie Cameron, he was a serious student of the esoteric, and may have blown himself up performing an occult ritual. As handsome as a movie star, Parsons is one of the most intriguing and charismatic of characters in L.A. occult history, or in all of L.A. history for that matter.

Israel Regardie (1907-1985) While living in Studio City, Regardie practiced as a chiropractor, neo-Reichian therapist, and as a Jungian trained in psychoanalysis. He wrote fourteen books, some of which exposed the secrets of Aleister Crowley and the Golden Dawn much to their dislike. He is widely considered to be one of the major occultists of the twentieth century.

Carroll Righter (1900-1988) One of the first celebrity astrologers who was reputed to be an advisor to President and Nancy Reagan. Righter wrote a daily astrology column that was syndicated to 166 newspapers around the world. He was the author of *Astrology and You* and other best-selling astrology books, and his Foundation has had ongoing astrology classes in Hollywood every Tuesday night since 1964.

Billboard of the Strange Angel series based on the life of Jack Parsons

HE BLEW HIMSELF UP, OR DID HE?

As handsome as a 40s movie star, Jack Parsons, (born Marvel Whiteside Parsons; 1914 – 1952), died at the age of thirty-seven in a horrific explosion which was either an accident, suicide, or assassination.

In his short life Parsons rose to prominence in two widely disparate arenas: as a major player in the history of the U.S. space program, and as one of L.A.'s and perhaps the world's most prominent occultists.

As a child, Jack Parsons's interest in sci-fi led him to experiment with rockets, later being expelled from boys' school for blowing up toilets. He went on to become one of the principal founders of Pasadena's Jet Propulsion Laboratory (JPL), where he invented the first rocket engine.

Parsons's obsession with the occult began in childhood as well: he performed rituals in his bedroom to invoke the Devil, stopping until later in life when he feared he was successful. In his search for occult knowledge it is known that Parsons attended lectures on Theosophy (see page 63) by Krishnamurti. At the age of twenty-five, he converted to the Thelema of Aleister Crowley (see page 86), heading the local OTO lodge in Pasadena.

Parsons's house in Pasadena, called The Parsonage, functioned as a commune and included a laboratory in the basement. Occult rituals were performed at the house, the most famous being the Babalon Working which was designed to bring the Scarlet Woman goddess to earth. Co-worker in this ritual was L. Ron Hubbard, the founder of Scientology. When Marjorie Cameron (see page 88), appeared at the house soon after, Hubbard and Parsons decided she was indeed the Scarlet Woman (it didn't hurt that she had red hair), and Parsons married her.

Perhaps due to karma, perhaps bad luck, Parsons's fortunes changed. An alcoholic and heavy user of cannabis, he had moved onto harder drugs. He was expelled from JPL for his hazardous conduct in the workplace and for his occult proclivities. He was under investigation by the FBI and the Pasadena police department and was accused of being a spy. Parson's father had died as a psychiatric patient hospitalized for severe clinical depression, which some authors have speculated Jack inherited. When Jack died from the explosion in the basement, it was either a science project gone wrong, an occult working, suicide, or an assassination for his alleged espionage activities.

Jack Parsons was a mad genius, an occultist, an author, someone who really was a "rocket scientist," an intrepid explorer of inner and outer space, and certainly one of Spiritual L.A.'s most fascinating characters.

The Parsonage

1003 S Orange Grove Ave (no longer exists), Pasadena, CA 9120

THE WICKEDEST MAN IN THE WORLD

Surely, you've heard of 666, the number of the Mark of the Beast? The reference is from the Book of Revelations of the Christian Bible and denotes the Devil or Satan. Aleister Crowley audaciously chose this number as his moniker.

Most if not all of modern Western occultism has been influenced by Aleister Crowley (1875 – 1947) and his religious philosophy of Thelema. He was a larger-than-life character of much theatricality, media-savvy, and drama, always with an eye to his historical legacy. Crowley was a prolific writer of articles, poetry, and books including *The Book of the Law*, ("Do What Thou Wilt Shall Be the Whole of the Law") and *Magick in Theory and Practice*. He was bisexual and had numerous wives and consorts, several of whom he christened the Scarlet Woman, a goddess who was a sexually-free woman. Crowley wrote at length about his sexual and drug addictions and his efforts to stop heroin.

Crowley's Thelema is a system of ceremonial *magick* (written with a "k" to differentiate it from stage and entertainment magic), beliefs and rituals intended to influence matter and develop the *magickian* personally and spiritually. Modern psychological tenets such as the use of affirmations, will, and intention all have *magickal* properties. Crowley visited L.A. in November, 1915 and described Angelenos as a "cinema crowd of cocaine-crazed sexual lunatics." (Like he should talk! Lol) His followers believe he was the Avatar of the New Age.

Aleister Crowley was famously an influence on Led Zeppelin, and his picture appeared on the cover of the Beatles' *Sgt. Pepper's Lonely Hearts Club Band*. Noted followers in Spiritual L.A. include Kenneth Anger, Cameron, Jack Parsons, Paul Foster Case and B.O.T.A., Israel Regardie, and Satanists of all persuasions. There are several local Thelema groups teaching and practicing *magick* -- you can find them on Meetup or by Googling Thelema or the Ordo Templi Orientis (OTO).

Some say L. Ron Hubbard (see page 42) and Scientology were heavily influenced by Aleister Crowley's work, although the Church denies it. It is, however, a fact that in 1945 Hubbard moved into Jack Parson (see page 84) 's Pasadena mansion and collaborated on a magickal ritual called the "Babalon Working." It is also true that Hubbard married Jack Parson's lover, Sara, (the sister of his wife), a noted Crowley-ite. Whether or not they defrauded Parsons of his life's savings when they eloped depends on who you ask.

Aleister Crowley died in poverty and addiction, but his myth and influence live on.

THE SCARLET WOMAN

A retrospective of Marjorie Cameron (1922 – 1995) 's artwork entitled "Cameron: Songs for the Witch Woman" was held at L.A.'s Museum of Contemporary Art in 2014. Although she had been established within the artistic and avant-garde communities for decades, it was only after her death that her reputation grew.

Before that time, Cameron, as she chose to be called, was perhaps most well-known as the wife of Jack Parsons, the infamous rocket scientist and occultist (see page 84). When she visited Parson's home in Pasadena after he and L. Ron Hubbard had been performing the Babalon Working (see page 234), her red hair made Parsons believe she was the Scarlet Woman prophesized by Aleister Crowley as one of the beacons of the new age. They married in 1946, and although they were frequently separated, they were together until he died in the freakish explosion in their home in 1952.

Cameron had been born and raised in the Midwest where her rebellious nature and artistic proclivities made her the black sheep of the family. She worked for the railroad, and enlisted in the navy for several years before she made it to L.A. Excelling as an artist, a writer, a poet and an actress, here Cameron found herself an active member of the avant-garde artists working at the intersection of art and drugs. She continued throughout the rest of her life to produce writings, poetry, drawings, and paintings, and acted as a mentor to such well-known artists as

Bronson Park

Wallace Berman and George Herms. Kenneth Anger (see page 82) had her star as The Scarlet Woman in his film *Inauguration of the Pleasure Dome*, the entirety of which can be watched on YouTube.

Nomadic, Cameron lived at various times in Pasadena, West Hollywood, Venice, Joshua Tree, Beaumont, Mexico, San Francisco, and Santa Fe. Later in life she suffered from poor physical and mental health, mostly due to heavy drug use. After moving back to L.A. she was often to be seen practicing tai chi in Bronson Park with the group around Marshal Ho'o. Cameron continued to believe she was Aleister Crowley's prophesized Scarlet Woman until the end of her days when she died in L.A. in 1995.

B.O.T.A.

I entered from the parking lot into the tiny kitchen where smatterings of junk food were laid out on paper plates for fellowship after the service. The door opened onto a large room with gleaming linoleum floors and about thirty people sitting on folding chairs, mostly middle-aged and solid-looking although in the back of the crowd sat two young hipsters. The sanctuary and altar were graced with colorful paintings of tarot cards, and a handful of robed participants were seated on the right. Quite a few closed doors around the hall led to other parts of the building.

The ceremony was solemn and organized much like the Protestant church services I attended as a child, although the content was, of course, quite different. The Reverend Ann Davies gave an uplifting, vaguely motivational sermon while the congregation chanted phrases one wouldn't hear outside these walls.

Builders of the Adytum (BOTA) was founded in L.A. by occultist Paul Foster Case (1884-1954) in 1922. BOTA has its roots in the Masons and the Golden Dawn with whom Case had a disagreement and left to start his own Mystery School. "Builders" stands for carpenters (like Jesus), and "Adytum" is Latin for "inner shrine."

BOTA is most noted for its correspondence courses that teach tarot, astrology, Qabalah (Kabbalah), meditation and other esoteric techniques. All beliefs are honored as part of the Ageless Wisdom, although Qabalah is seen as the base of both Judaism and Christianity. Most of Paul Foster Case's writings can be found on the Internet for free as part of the public domain.

The physical location in Highland Park offers healing work and rituals for its members. There are offices and a gift shop. The work has been continued by Reverend Davies, under whose guidance BOTA has flourished and spread to Australia and Europe.

Builders of the Adytum

Although the service seemed middle-class-safe and even a bit sleepy, one has to wonder what is going on behind all those doors? What is the meaning of the chants and robes? What secrets is BOTA in touch with? A lovely shroud of mystery hung over the whole affair.

On the way out, I approached the young hipsters and asked what they thought, assuming unfairly they'd react judgmentally. "As a serious student of the occult," the man said as his kohl-eyed companion nodded, "I like a lot of what they're up to."

Builders of the Adytum

5101 N Figueroa St, Los Angeles, CA 90042

Templo Santa Muerte

THE DARK SIDE

The tantric perspective is that all is spiritual; all is divine. The light cannot exist without the dark; they are two sides of the same coin. No guide to Spiritual L.A. would be complete without a visit to the dark side, a place where many worship.

Of course, we have the whole magickal tradition as practiced by Jack Parsons, Cameron, and Kenneth Anger, which many designate as black magic. Some consider the Church of Scientology to be up to something demonic. Fingers can be found pointing at just about anything as wrong, dark, or bad -- depends which side you're on. The following L.A. institutions are either intriguing or "evil," depending on your point of view:

Devil's Gate

The original Tongva people warned us: The place has bad energy. They forbid their people to move too close to the Devil's Face outcropping in the rocks. They claimed that the sound of the rapids rushing through the gorge was the sound of the coyote spirit laughing.

Behind the Devil's Gate Dam in Pasadena is a concrete tunnel covered in graffiti that may be nothing other than what it is or, some say, a portal to hell. According to legend, Aleister Crowley (see page 86) recognized the location's occult power, and Jack Parsons and L. Ron Hubbard performed a ritual to open a "hell portal," or a gateway to another dimension that allows negative energies and otherworldly entities to pass through.

The profile of the devil can be made out in the rocks, and the water flowing through the gates does, maybe, sound like it's laughing. Some hikers report stumbling upon people performing Satanic rituals *"but they're really nice."* (Yelp)

La Cañada Flintridge, CA 91011

The Satanic Temple

A national group, the Los Angeles Division was formed in 2016 and has about 50 members. They claim they don't actually worship Satan but see him as a rebel saint advocating for personal freedom and independence. The national organization's headquarters is in Salem, Massachusetts, where in the seventeenth century twenty people were executed as witches. You can find the locals on their Facebook page.

Facebook: The Satanic Temple Southern California: Los Angeles Division

Templo Santa Muerte

A rapidly growing movement worshipping "Holy Death," this group began in Mexico and Central America ministering to drug dealers, prostitutes, crime lords, murderers and thieves who are also devout Catholics. The local temple is a one-room storefront with a botanica next door selling candles and other offerings. *Santa Muerte* is depicted as a female skeleton wearing colorful garments.

4902 Melrose Ave, Los Angeles, CA 90004

TRADITIONAL RELIGIONS

TRADITIONAL RELIGIONS IN L.A.

With our independent streak and tendency toward identifying as "spiritual but not religious," traditional religions have not been as strong in L.A. as elsewhere in the country. In 1906, for example, it was estimated that only thirty-five percent of California's population belonged to a church compared to seventy percent of the rest of the country. This does not mean, of course, that traditional religions do not provide deep spiritual sustenance for many, many Angelenos. Of course they do.

About sixty-five percent of L.A. identifies as Christian, three percent Jewish, three percent Muslim, two percent Buddhist, and Other Faiths or Nothing twenty-six percent (includes agnostics, atheists, "spiritual but not religious," and "don't know").

Racial discrimination against non-whites has, unfortunately, been very strong in L.A.; however, there has been a surprising lack of religious intolerance. Far less tension exists between Catholics and Protestants than in the East, and the spiritual tenets and customs of Blacks, Jews, Muslims, and Asians have been treated on more or less equal footing with their Catholic neighbors.

The Catholic Church

Priests from the Mission San Gabriel established L.A.'s first church, The Church of Our Lady Queen of the Angels as a sub-mission. It remained L.A.'s only Catholic church for many years.

Today there are about four million Catholics in L.A. attending services at roughly three hundred churches. These are primarily Latino but include services held in forty different languages.

Unfortunately, there have been a record-breaking numbers of cases of Catholic clergy sexual abuse that are still not settled to this day.

Protestants

The New England ministers who came to California cherished the idea of remaking their religions as they saw fit. They tended to be personalities who gravitated to the new, to independence and freedom of thought.

The first Protestant church in L.A was First Congregational Church of Los Angeles, established in 1867. Various denominations settled into different geographic areas: Methodists in Long Beach, German Presbyterians founded Anaheim, and other Presbyterians and Methodists chose Pasadena and established it as a temperance (no alcohol) town. Mormons settled in San Bernardino.

Of the sixty-five percent Christians in L.A., Protestants are made up of eighteen percent Evangelicals, nine percent Mainline Protestants, and three percent Historically Black Protestants. Jehovah's Witness are one percent.

Photo right: First A.M.E. Protestant Church

FIRST
AME CHURCH
FIRST A.M.E. CHURCH

TEN FAMOUS CHURCHES AND TEMPLES IN L.A.

Cathedral of Our Lady of Angels

Completed in 2002, the seat of the L.A. Roman Catholic Archdiocese. There are little finds all over the place – holy relics, statues, paintings, the garden. The modern architecture is loved by many, not so (vehemently) by others. What's your vote?

555 W Temple St, Los Angeles, CA 90012

First African Methodist Episcopal (AME) Church of Los Angeles

Began in 1872, this is the oldest church founded by African Americans in Los Angeles. It counts more than nineteen thousand members.

2270 Harvard, Los Angeles, CA 90018

Good Shepherd Church

Famous because of the worldwide fascination with the seventeen-year old Elizabeth Taylor whose wedding to the heir to the Hilton fortune was held here in 1950. Can you say *paparazzi*?

504 N Roxbury Dr, Beverly Hills, CA 90210

Hollywood United Methodist Church

You've seen it on your way to the Hollywood Bowl - the church on the corner of Highland and Franklin with the HIV/AIDS red ribbon on it. (Insider tip – the parking lot is open for Bowl goers and your fee is a donation to the church.)

6817 Franklin Ave, Los Angeles, CA 90028

Holy Transfiguration Russian Orthodox Cathedral

Been curious about that fabulous "castle" you can see off the 101 near Fountain and Western? Well, now you know-- it's one of L.A.'s three Russian Orthodox churches.

5432 Fernwood Ave, Los Angeles, CA 90027

Photo left: Holy Transfiguration Russian Orthodox Cathedral

Cathedral of Our Lady of Angels

"La Placita" – The Church of Our Lady Queen of the Angels (El Pueblo de Nuestra Señora Reina de los Angeles)

L.A.'s first church founded in 1784 only three years after the official birthdate of Los Angeles. Across the street from El Pueblo de Los Angeles (home of Olvera Street).

535 N Main St, Los Angeles, CA 90012

Los Angeles California Temple

That sprawling lawn, that gorgeous temple – the second largest LDS (Mormon) temple in the world. You can get a grounds pass, but you can't go inside to glimpse the secrets you want to see.

10777 Santa Monica Blvd, Los Angeles, CA 90025

Malibu Hindu Temple

Almost like in India, well maybe not. If you go at the right time, you might be welcomed to a ceremony that includes chanting and pouring milk over statues.

1600 Las Virgenes Canyon Rd, Calabasas, CA 91302

Mosaic Church

Movement begun in L.A. Now has seven locations. Christian, evangelical, into music, was once housed in a nightclub.

7107 Hollywood Blvd, Los Angeles, CA 90046

Oasis Church

Noted for sponsoring a star on the Hollywood Walk of Fame for Jesus Christ. Famous church members have included Donna Summer, disco queen, and Viola Davis, Oscar-winning actor.

634 Normandie Ave, Los Angeles, CA 90005

Thien Hau Temple

Chinatown temple known for its beauty, dedicated to the sea goddess, Mazu.

756 Yale St, Los Angeles, CA 90012

West Angeles Church of God in Christ

Evangelical Christian church with twenty-four thousand members. z

3045 Crenshaw Blvd, Los Angeles, CA 90016

Malibu Hindu Temple

HOLY COW

Looming above the altar? A six-foot painting of a cow where the crucifix should be. The large vacant space appeared to hold the aftermath of a party, which is exactly what it was. The friendly manager told us that last evening's event had been one in which revelers ate as much meat as possible, without utensils, rubbing their greasy hands all over each other's... well, you may or may not get the picture. My friend and I had wandered in off the street to check out St. Vibiana's church and found it had been turned into an event space.

St. Vibiana's was the official cathedral of L. A. for over one hundred years. Developers wanted to tear it down, but the building survives and now hosts Emmy Awards parties, weddings, and American Idol episodes. On the side street is the trendy restaurant with five-star reviews, Redbird.

The relics of the third-century Christian martyr, Saint Vibiana, had been housed there, enclosed in a marble sarcophagus. The remains have been moved to The Cathedral of Our Lady of the Angels, which in 2002 became the official Catholic Church of Los Angeles.

Vibiana

214 S Main St, Los Angeles, CA 90012

L'CHAIM!

Along Melrose or La Brea on Friday nights, you might see a parade of men dressed in medieval black with circular fur hats, their wives behind them wearing wigs or other head coverings – Orthodox Jews en route to celebrate Shabbat, the Jewish day of rest. They travel on foot because they will not drive cars or perform other activities designated as work during the time lasting from a few minutes before sundown on Friday to Saturday night.

L.A. is home to the second-largest Jewish population in the U.S. (after New York City) numbering over six hundred thousand. Jews first arrived in 1841 and mainly settled downtown around Temple Street, which became known as the "Jewish district." Eventually Boyle Heights housed the largest Jewish community, while the major migration after World War II concentrated in West L.A. and Encino. Another exodus of Persian Jews came in the 70s after the revolution in Iran.

Around L.A. you'll encounter highly visible Jewish landmarks such as Cedars-Sinai Medical Center, the Skirball Cultural Center, and the lively communities of Persian shops and restaurants along Westwood Boulevard and Ventura Boulevard in Encino. Prominent Jewish leaders created the Hollywood film industry and the city of Beverly Hills. Some of the most well-known mid-century modern architects were Jewish, among them Austrian immigrants Richard Neutra and Rudolph Schindler, and of course our home town hero, Frank Gehry. Eric Garcetti is our first Jewish mayor.

Special mention must be made of L.A.'s fabulous Jewish delis. Langer's Delicatessen was named America's #1 Deli by *Food & Wine* magazine. Canter's Deli is the twenty-four-hour restaurant known also for its thriving after-hours scene of rock 'n' roll and other musicians. A plaque hangs over Rodney Bingenheimer's booth, the KROQ jock who introduced us to Guns N'Roses, the Sex Pistols, and Blondie among numerous others.

MAJOR JEWISH TEMPLES:

Wilshire Boulevard Temple (oldest in L.A.)

3663 Wilshire Blvd, Los Angeles, CA 90010

Chabad of Malibu

22943 Pacific Coast Hwy, Malibu, CA 90265

Leo Baeck Temple

1300 N Sepulveda Blvd, Los Angeles, CA 90049

Temple Israel of Hollywood

7300 Hollywood Blvd, Los Angeles, CA 90046

MAJOR LANDMARKS:

American Jewish University

15600 Mulholland Dr, Los Angeles, CA 90077

Cedar-Sinai Medical Center

8700 Beverly Blvd, Los Angeles, CA 90048

Los Angeles Museum of the Holocaust

100 The Grove Dr, Los Angeles, CA 90036

Skirball Cultural Center

2701 N Sepulveda Blvd, Los Angeles, CA 90049

Canter's Deli

SPECIAL MENTION:

Canter's Deli

419 N Fairfax Ave, Los Angeles, CA 90036

Langer's Delicatessen

704 S Alvarado St, Los Angeles, CA 90057

OUR NEWEST FRIENDS

Of all the major world religions, Islam has the second-largest number of believers, and it is the third-largest religion in the United States. Most people think of Islam as belonging to the Middle East, but in fact only twenty percent live there. Most Muslims live in Indonesia, India, Pakistan, and Africa.

Los Angeles is home to half a million Muslims (second only to New York City). Since 1965 L.A. has attracted more Muslim Immigrants than any other city. After the Revolution in Iran in 1979 an influx of Persian Muslims arrived. The first mosque in L.A. was the Islamic Center of Southern California, which was founded in 1952. Today L.A. is the home to over 120 mosques.

Los Angeles is abundant with the rich contributions of its Muslim citizens. A few prominent celebrities are Mahershala Ali, the two-time Academy award-winning actor and rapper, Mohamed Hadid, real-estate developer and father of top models Gigi and Bella, Ice Cube, rapper and producer, and Reza Aslan, the author, religious scholar, and host of the show *Believer.* Shirin Neshat, the Iranian-American artist and film director, does not live in L.A. but deserves an honorable mention as The Broad art museum recently featured the largest exhibition of her work to-date.

King Fahad Mosque

MAJOR MOSQUES:

Islamic Center of Southern California

434 Vermont Ave, Los Angeles, CA 90020

King Fahad Mosque

10980 Washington Blvd, Culver City, CA 90232

Masjid Umar Ibn Al-Khattab

1025 W Exposition Blvd, Los Angeles, CA 90007

THE SPIRITUAL AWAKENING OF THE 60s & 70s

TOUR

WESTSIDE SPIRITUAL L.A.

1 The Lake Shrine

Calm, meditative, peaceful – sheer joy. Don't forget the gift shop.

17190 Sunset Blvd, Pacific Palisades, CA 90272

Carlos Castaneda's Haunts

Tour previous places this spiritual rockstar lived and studied (see page 123)

2 The Feminist Wicca (previous site)

442 Lincoln Blvd, Venice, CA 90291

3 Hare Krishna Temple and Govinda's Restaurant

Be sure to eat lunch here.

3764 Watseka Ave, Los Angeles, CA 90034

4 The Kabbalah Center

Where Madonna and Britney got their red strings.

1062 S Robertson Blvd, Los Angeles, CA 90035

5 **Kuruvugna Springs**

Only open the first Saturdays of the month. Check their Facebook page to see if they're open this particular first Saturday. (see page 13)

1439 S Barrington Ave, Los Angeles, CA 90025

6 **Thunderbolt Books**

The store has a rich history: Carlos Castaneda and others used to hold classes upstairs.

512 Santa Monica Blvd, Santa Monica, CA 90401

7 **Tongva Park**

We took their land; we can at least give them back a park. Note several sculptures that are modern interpretations of the Tongva dwellings seen at Kuruvugna or in one of the museums.

1615 Ocean Ave, Santa Monica, CA 90401

Venice on a weekday (see page 168)

Thunderbolt Books

Photo right: The Lake Shrine

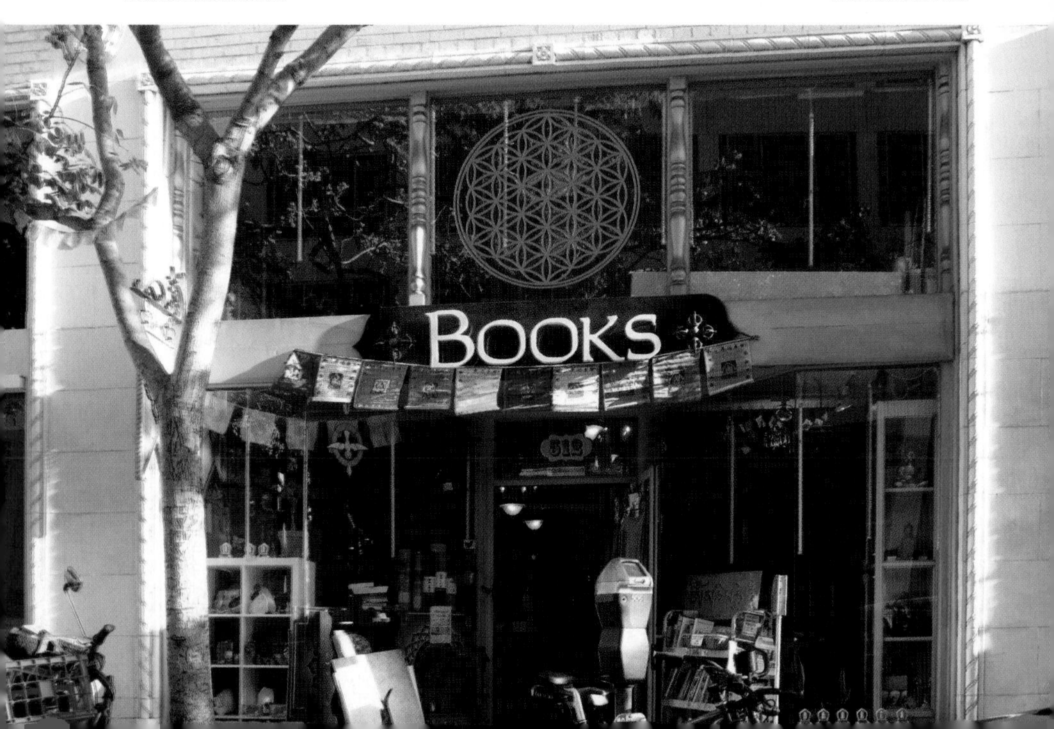

WESTSIDE SPIRITUAL L.A.

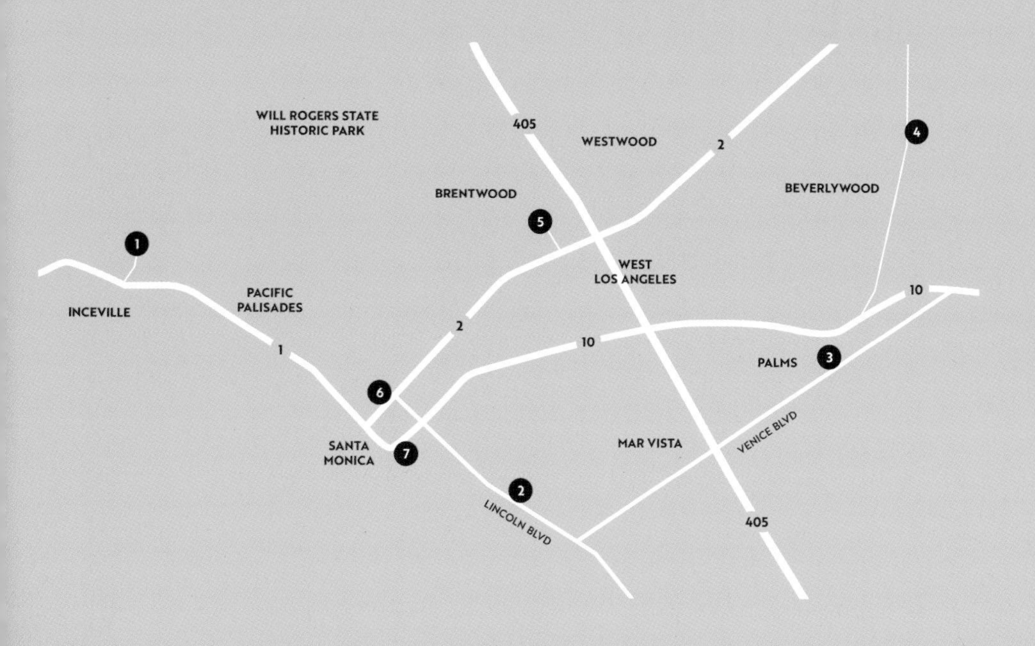

The (former) Mother House

FATHER YOD AND THE SOURCE FAMILY

In the Oscar-winning Best Picture, *Annie Hall*, Woody Allen famously orders, "... the alfalfa sprouts and a plate of mashed yeast." His commentary on L.A. cuisine was voiced at The Source, one of the country's first health food restaurants and a 70s fixture on the Sunset Strip.

The Source was a gathering place for Hollywood royalty such as John Lennon, Frank Zappa, Julie Christie and countless others, reporting to gross up to $10K a day at its peak. The staff took part in group meditations before and after their shifts and lived communally as the Source Family in a Hollywood Hills mansion called The Mother House.

The charismatic founder of the Family and the restaurant was Jim Baker, an ex-Marine who took the name Father Yod (pronounced yode). Yod sported a white beard and white suits, was chauffeured about in a Rolls-Royce, had 14 "spiritual wives," and led the Family's psychedelic rock band, Ya Ho Wa 13, whose sixty-five albums are now highly-prized collectors' items.

The Family embodied one of the most enduring stereotypes of LA: good-looking, health-food-eating young people, meditating and doing yoga, enjoying casual sex while listening to the groovy music of the time. On the Internet you can find intriguing photos of all 150 of them wearing floor-length white robes lounging around the mansion, or holding hands in a long human chain along the beach in Malibu.

The unconventional behavior of the family attracted scrutiny from authorities and thus the Family relocated to Hawaii in 1974. In 1975, Father Yod died in a hang-gliding accident (he went up with no previous experience), and the group dispersed. However, even today former Family members still talk about how their lives were positively shaped by this shared adventure, and a fascinating documentary, The Source Family, was released in 2012. Highly recommended for a psychedelic time travel to when alternative spirituality went almost mainstream.

The (former) Mother House

2411 Inverness Ave, Los Angeles, CA 90027

The Source Restaurant (now Cabo Cantina)

8301 Sunset Blvd, West Hollywood, CA 90069

FLIRTY FISHING

In 1968, during the height of the hippie and sexual liberation era, a group of Jesus freaks began baptizing new converts near the Huntington Beach pier. Four years later, by 1972, the Children of God had moved to Laurel Canyon and expanded to include one hundred and thirty communes around the world. At its peak it claimed eighteen thousand members.

How did they grow so quickly? Part of their recruiting method was sending missionaries to foreign countries, part was proselytizing in the streets and selling pamphlets, and part was a form of religious prostitution called "flirty fishing."

The cult was headed by their charismatic leader, David Berg (1919-1994), who liked to be referred to as Moses and communicated with his followers in a series of three thousand "Mo Letters." His teaching was a bizarre mix of Christian fundamentalism and unconventional (to say the least) sexuality. Until the late 80s, the Children of God openly advocated prostitution and incest with minors, believing that children should be initiated by adults, often their parents.

Female members of the Children of God were expected to raise money for the cult and gain new converts by having sex with them. In addition to the term "flirty fishing," this was called "Hooking for Jesus" or "God's Whores." The flirty fishers "practiced their ministry" in the hippie community, in stores, discotheques and clubs. Women were expected to have sex daily with different men in and out of the cult, even if they were married. Contraception was forbidden, so many children referred to as "Jesus babies" were born. Flirty fishing was discontinued by the church in 1987 due to the AIDS crisis and the ensuing worldwide-changed attitude toward casual sex.

The (former) Laurel Canyon compound

Famous members of the Children of God were Rose McGowan, two early Fleetwood Mac members, and the family of River and Joaquin Phoenix. River Phoenix was an Academy Award-nominated actor who died of a drug overdose in 1993 in front of the Viper Room at the age of twenty-three.

The cult changed its name to The Family International in 2004 and is headed by Karen Zerby, Berg's widow. It currently has seventeen hundred members in eighty different countries. The website states, "Although we no longer practice FFing [flirty fishing], we believe the scriptural principles behind the ministry remain sound."

The Laurel Canyon compound of The Children of God was at:

1821 Oakden Dr, Los Angeles. CA 90046

"TURN ON, TUNE IN, AND DROP OUT"

Timothy Leary (1920 – 1996) was one of the most prominent figures of the 60s counterculture. Originally from the East Coast, Leary lived in L.A. from 1976 until his death in 1996.

Leary was most famous as a loud, vocal proponent of LSD. It may seem strange in a day when acid is mostly considered one of a smorgasbord of festival drugs, but in the 60s, it was advocated as an aid in spiritual search. Leary, along with colleagues, wrote *The Psychedelic Experience* comparing tripping to *The Tibetan Book of the Dead*, and in 1966, founded the League for Spiritual Discovery, a religion declaring LSD as its holy sacrament.

Fired from his professorship at Harvard for researching the therapeutic possibilities of psychedelics (along with Richard Alpert, now widely known as the spiritual teacher, Ram Dass), Leary appeared frequently in the media advocating for the right of individuals to explore our own minds. He was arrested numerous times on bogus drug charges because he was considered a threat to the status quo, culminating with Richard Nixon proclaiming him "the most dangerous man in America."

Later, Leary performed in colleges and nightclubs as a "stand-up philosopher" and was an early adopter and proponent of computers and their possibility for mind expansion. He hung out with numerous celebrities including Johnny Depp, Aldous Huxley, Dan Aykroyd, and Allen Ginsberg and was often seen around L.A. at trendy hot spots.

"Chromatic Cascade"
street art by Jen Stark

Certainly, due to Timothy Leary's influence, many have used psychedelic drugs in their spiritual search and found meaning there. His life and work influenced many people to explore altered states of consciousness and alternative religious movements.

Timothy Leary previously lived at:

10106 Sunbrook Dr, Beverly Hills, CA 90210

Psychedelic Street Art:

"Chromatic Cascade" by Jen Stark

1825 Conway Pl, Los Angeles, CA 90021

OH HAPPY DAY

Meanwhile in South Central, L.A. was blossoming as a world center of sacred music. During the 60s and 70s, giants in the pantheon of gospel introduced this spiritual music into the realm of popular culture, and the world has never been the same.

What we know today as gospel music is a blend of various elements of African American culture. Its roots are in West Africa where music was considered a potent connector to the spirit world, utilizing call and response singing, drums, and dance. After Africans were forced into slavery in the U.S., they merged this indigenous music with Christian hymns to form what was at the time referred to as "Negro Spirituals." A form of worship also developed called "shouts" in which participants would shuffle in the center of a circle of musicians when they felt the spirit.

Like Pentecostalism, gospel music was not born in L.A. but came to prominence here. Thomas A. Dorsey (1899-1993) from Chicago is considered the Father of Gospel music. However, when William J. Seymour's preaching at the Bonnie Brae House (see page 72) and the following Azusa Street Revival sowed the seeds for the worldwide Pentecostal movement in 1906, the staid hymns of traditional Christian churches were not a match for the exuberance of these new congregations. And so, a new form of African American sacred music evolved.

In 1967, gospel burst onto the international Top Singles charts around the world with "Oh Happy Day" by the Edwin Hawkins Singers (if you haven't heard this song, put this book down, open Spotify and listen RIGHT NOW). Thus was born the new category of Contemporary Gospel.

L.A. producers James Cleveland and Andraé Crouch were two giants of the Contemporary Gospel scene. James Cleveland (1931-1991), also called the Prince of Gospel, produced more than one hundred and ninety albums, wrote and performed some of its most well-loved songs, and founded the Gospel Workshop of America, an annual convention nurturing many talented artists. He recorded Aretha Franklin's *Amazing Grace*, the best-selling gospel album of all time.

Andraé Crouch (1942-2015) had a massive impact on religious music worldwide. He and his twin sister, Sandra Crouch (1942- present), multi-Grammy-winner in her own right, grew up in Pacoima and were initially Pentecostal. He is widely credited with bringing spiritual music into the mainstream and helping to bridge the gap between Black and White. Crouch worked with Madonna on *Like a Prayer* and with Michael Jackson on his albums, *Bad*, *Dangerous* and *History*, as well as with Elvis, Elton John, and Paul Simon.

New Christ Memorial Church

Another L.A. gospel star was Della Reese (1931-2017), a prominent singer, actress, talk show host, New Thought minister (see page 138) and founder of her own The Up Church in Inglewood. The now defunct House of Blues on Sunset used to host a celebratory and always-sold-out Sunday Gospel Brunch. You can still get tickets in Anaheim, Las Vegas, or San Diego, or further east in Houston, Chicago, or Orlando.

Currently, GospoCentric Records in Inglewood is one of the most prominent gospel labels, hosting Kirk Franklin and Mary Mary, who have brought urban flavor to gospel. Sandra Crouch continues on as the Pastor of New Christ Memorial Church in San Fernando leading services each Sunday.

Gospel would not be as prominent today if not for its flowering in Los Angeles in the 60s and 70s. L.A.'s gospel music has brought faith, joy, and sustenance to millions worldwide.

New Christ Memorial Church

13333 Vaughn St, San Fernando, CA 91340

The UP Church

600 Queen St, Inglewood, CA 90301

DRUGS, BRUJOS, SHAPESHIFTING, AND THE WITCHES

One of the rock stars of L.A. spirituality was the great sorcerer himself, Carlos Castaneda, (born in Peru in 1925, died in Westwood in 1998) who brought the use of psychedelic drugs for personal and spiritual growth to the attention of the mainstream. His twelve books still sell well today and to date have sold more than twenty-eight million copies, which catapulted Carlos Castaneda to international fame.

Castaneda's books, the first of which was *The Teachings of Don Juan: A Yaqui Way of Knowledge*, are an account of his apprenticeship in Toltec shamanism. The early books were written for his Ph.D. in anthropology at UCLA. They are full of colorful tales of such miracles as people turning into crows, talking to coyotes, jumping off cliffs and surviving, and disappearing into thin air and reappearing elsewhere. There is much ingesting of herbs, mushrooms and cacti, and while in these states, Don Juan imparts higher knowledge to Carlos.

This higher knowledge is of a "nonordinary" or a "separate" reality," of the ways to personal and spiritual power, and of how to become a "warrior." Whether or not the books are fictional has been a big controversy, but there is no doubt that learning about the "Yaqui way of knowledge" has raised the consciousness of countless people worldwide whether or not the facts are "true."

Castaneda abandoned public life in 1973 and disappeared from view, refusing to be photographed. He lived quietly in Westwood with the three "witches:" Florinda Donner-Grau, Taisha Abelar, and Carol Tiggs, women of power who practiced shamanism and wrote fascinating books of their own. He reappeared in the 90s to teach Tensegrity, a series of spiritual exercises based on ancient Toltec sources.

Detroit Street

Pandora Ave.

Carlos Castaneda died in his home in Westwood in 1998. The witches mysteriously disappeared, leaving no trace. All their phone numbers were reportedly disconnected on the same day. Many speculated they had committed group suicide although only one body was found. Some believed they had left this reality to enter a "separate reality" with Carlos.

The best place to get more information about Castaneda and the witches is at the Sustained Action website.

DRIVE-BYS OF PLACES IN THE LIFE OF CARLOS CASTANEDA

Castaneda attended Los Angeles City College:

📍 ***855 N Vermont Ave, Los Angeles, CA 90029***

He received his Ph.D. at the UCLA Department of Anthropology:

📍 ***375 Portola Plaza, Los Angeles, CA 90095***

Carlos previously lived at:

📍 ***823 S Detroit St, Los Angeles, CA 90036***

Castaneda and the witches lived at this complex from 1973 until his death in 1998:

📍 ***1672 Pandora Ave, Los Angeles, CA 90024***

Sunday Sessions were held at Dance Home:

📍 ***522 Santa Monica Blvd, Santa Monica, CA 90401***

Castaneda taught classes upstairs at Thunderbolt Books (previously Phoenix):

📍 ***512 Santa Monica Blvd, Santa Monica, CA 90401***

Cleargreen, Incorporated

Cleargreen was established to carry on Castaneda's teachings, particularly Tensegrity, or Magical Passes, based on a Toltec discipline of spiritually powerful exercises. The staff there told me that at least one of the witches is alive and well and shows up at the Center regularly.

📍 ***10812A Washington Blvd, Culver City, CA 90232***

Z FOR ZSUZSANNA

In 1975, a sting was arranged by an undercover policewoman against a lone tarot card reader at her store in Venice, California, "The Feminist Wicca." It is hard to believe, but only such a short time ago practicing "fortune-telling," including tarot, astrology, and psychic readings, was against the law.

Zsuzsanna Budapest (born 1940 in Budapest, Hungary), more simply referred to as "Z," is a leading figure in feminist spirituality and Wicca. She is the author of numerous books and articles including *The Feminist Book of Lights and Shadows* and *The Holy Book of Women's Mysteries*. Now in her eighties, she leads rituals, workshops, classes, and is an activist and the President of the Women's Spirituality Forum. Many teachers and writers of the Goddess religion cite her work as a major influence.

Z and her lawyers described her 1975 arrest as "the first witch prosecuted since Salem." When she was found guilty, they proceeded on to the Supreme Court of California on the position that Wicca is a bona fide religion. After nine years of appeals the verdict was finally reversed as unconstitutional and as a violation of the Freedom of Religion Act. It is because of Z that the laws against fortune telling in California were struck down.

Z's mother was a medium, a practicing witch, and a sculptor in Hungary, and Z had been raised in the goddess religion. She moved to Chicago in 1959 where she studied at the famous Second City improvisational theater, and where she was married with two sons before she came out as a lesbian. Z moved to L. A. in 1970, and in addition to her store on Lincoln, was active at the Women's Center and in the Women's Liberation Movement. She currently lives in Santa Cruz County.

Previous site of The Feminist Wicca

442 Lincoln Blvd, Venice, CA 90291

THE CHURCH OF SYNANON

“Our religious posture is: Don't mess with us. You can get killed dead, literally dead... These are real threats ... I am quite willing to break some lawyer's legs, and next break his wife's legs, and threaten to cut their child's arm off ... I really do want an ear in a glass of alcohol on my desk." In 1978, LAPD reported a tape recording of Synanon founder, Chuck Dederich, stating the above in response to its investigation. Dederich, reportedly sober for decades, was arrested drunk later that year.

What happened? Synanon, like most cults, began with an inspired vision of helping humanity –this one by providing treatment for drug addicts. The founder, Dederich, had been an active member of AA who saw things differently after taking LSD and who created his own program. He is said to have been the one who coined the phrase, "Today is the first day of the rest of your life."

The Church of Synanon purchased a prime beachfront property in Santa Monica in 1967 and occupied it until 1978. The Church thrived during this time serving drug addicts in their residential programs, at one point generating up to $10 million a year (in 70s dollars, mind you).

Synanon became infamous for its highly-confrontive “therapeutic” method called “The Game.” A member would sit in the middle of a group, open up and talk about themselves, and then be vehemently criticized by the other group members, yelling and swearing, sometimes violently, for up to seventy-two hours. Hard to believe now, but during the heyday of the human potential movement in the 60s and 70s, Synanon techniques were treated as viable treatment methods.

Women residents were required to shave their heads, and many men were forced to get vasectomies. As in many cults, members ceased contact with their families. There were mass weddings, reported forced abortions, and married couples who were made to break up and join with new partners.

Hotel Casa del Mar

The 1965 big-budget Hollywood film "Synanon" grossed over a million dollars. On eBay you can still find Synanon record albums made by prominent jazz musicians, and all kinds of Synanon swag such as belt buckles, ballpoint pens, and memoirs of growing up in the cult.

Synanon disbanded in the late '80s amid allegations of murder and tax evasion, and Chuck Diderich's breakdown. The Church was formally dissolved in 1991 except for one remaining outpost in Germany.

However, as with all cults, there are those who credit it with saving their lives. There walk among us people alive today who credit the work of Synanon with curing their addictions.

Hotel Casa del Mar (Church of Synanon 1967-1978)

1910 Ocean Way, Santa Monica, CA 90405

MSIA

Another home-grown L.A. spiritual organization is the Movement of Spiritual Inner Awareness (MSIA). Founded in 1971 by John-Roger (born Roger Hinkins) (September 24, 1934 - October 22, 2014). MSIA is based in L.A. and is active mostly in the U.S. with an estimated 5,000 followers.

The more I looked into MSIA the more perplexed I became. I have no doubt they are doing good things for a number of people. One of my patients is enrolled in their year-long correspondence program and reports that she finds it extremely helpful. However, in all my research, I never came across any other group as secretive and non-transparent as it is except maybe the Church of Scientology. The degree of obfuscation is puzzling.

At age 29, the future John-Roger, or J-R as he was called, underwent surgery for a kidney stone during which time he fell into a nine-day coma and had a near-death experience. During this interlude he experienced higher consciousness in himself and changed his name and his life mission.

MSIA offers meditation techniques, discourses on spiritual practices and beliefs, a 12-year subscription study program, and emphasis on service to others. Each student receives a personal sound mantra similar to Transcendental Meditation (TM). The teachings are based on those of Christ, Buddha, and the Sant Mat/Radkasomit tradition which also influenced Eckankar and the Divine Light Mission.

The growth of MSIA was facilitated by the addition of its conventionally-handsome Spiritual Director, John Morton, who teaches, creates workshops, coaches, consults and writes. Both he and J-R are referred to as "The Traveler," a mystical figure who appears on the earth every 25,000 years.

MSIA has profoundly influenced many, but others who have left consider it a mind-manipulating cult. They state that J-R considered himself more powerful than Jesus Christ.

Whatever the truth, John-Roger and MSIA have created much good, including the Peace Awareness Labyrinth and Gardens (see page 152), the University of Santa Monica (see page 156), Insight Seminars, Heartfelt Foundation, and Mandeville Press.

SPIRITUALITY IN A SPEEDO

Posing in his Speedo, his chiseled dancer's body the very epitome of a Greek Adonis, Michel was a charismatic teacher who transmitted "The Knowing" to a group of 150-200 followers in weekly sessions in West Hollywood in the mid-to-late 1980s. At the height of the yuppie era, a cult flourished around him, living together 24/7 and calling themselves The Buddhafield. The cult members were decidedly not inclusive: all were white, slender, tall, conventionally good-looking – not a single person of color or average body shape (except for the filmmaker's sister), or interesting or alternative looks.

Will Allen, one of The Buddhafield members and the personal assistant and lover of Michel, made home movies at the time, not realizing that later he would turn them into the fascinating CNN documentary, *Holy Hell.*

When you watch the film, it is undeniable that something of a truly spiritual nature is happening: a sincere expression of love and radiance, the transmission of *shakti* energy. On the other hand, it is undeniable that you'll also see things of a decidedly weird nature as well. Such as:

Michel had previously been a dancer with the Oakland Ballet and a bit actor in movies, and, it was later unearthed, porn. He had the cult practice and stage elaborate ballets which were performed once and never for the public.

As a hypnotherapist Michel gave weekly, mandatory "cleansing" sessions costing fifty dollars (equivalent of one hundred fifty today), and during these sessions, he had regular sex with quite a few of the male devotees. This was either "sexual abuse" or "consensual sex" depending on whom you talk to.

After the news of this and allegations of brainwashing and manipulation, many of the twenty-year members left, feeling betrayed and wondering why they had participated in such cult-like behavior. They tell stories of not being allowed to watch TV, read books, have sex, listen to the radio, or own dogs.

What is truly fascinating, though, is that despite all this, all interviewed feel their experience in the cult had been worth it.

The Buddhafield moved to Austin, Texas in 1991, and Michel changed his name to Andreas. Today the cult is going one-hundred-person strong at Lanikai Beach in Hawaii, and Michel is now known by the name Reyji which means "God-King." Some of the longtime followers are still with him, as well as new devotees joining all the time.

For a delectable look at Spiritual L.A. history, the film *Holy Hell* is utterly compelling.

ANSWERING THE QUESTION: WHO ARE THOSE ALL-WHITE TURBAN PEOPLE?

You've seen them – the people wearing all-white with turbans -- haven't you? They keep to themselves but seem friendly and unabashed to be walking around looking like that. They are devotees of Yogi Bhajan, father of Kundalini Yoga in the U.S. A lively community thrives at Yoga West, their headquarters in L.A., teaching yoga classes and workshops.

Yogi Bhajan (born Harbhajan Singh Puri), (1929 – 2004) came to L.A. in 1968 and started the 3HO (Healthy, Happy, Holy Organization) Foundation out of an antique store on the corner of Robertson and Melrose. The organization now reports over 300 centers in 35 countries. His message was one of healthy living, family values, no drugs, vegetarianism, not cutting hair or beards, and advocating for peace and social justice. Kundalini Yoga as taught by Yogi Bhajan combines meditation, hatha yoga, breathing exercises, and mantra singing.

Gurmukh, one of Yogi Bhajan's most famous students, led Golden Bridge Yoga on Highland from 1993-2014, where she attracted such glitterati as Russell Brand, Demi Moore, Gabby Bernstein, and Madonna. One of the most popular Kirtan singers today is the movement's Snatam Kaur, whose voice and devotional music are not to be missed.

In early 2020, with the publication of former inner-circle member Pamela Dyson's book, *Premka: White Bird in a Golden Cage: My Life with Yogi Bhajan*, it came to light that Yogi Bhajan, in addition to serving as a powerful spiritual teacher to many, had been sexually abusing women for years. Reports by at least sixteen women of sexual, emotional, and physical abuse began pouring in. Many interviewed claim that this violence had been covered up for years, and indeed a *Time* magazine article written in

Yoga West

1977 characterized Yogi Bhajan as a "womanizer." You can watch a quite frightening video on YouTube from 1978 in which Yogi Bhajan states:

"Rape is always invited, it never happens. A person who is raped is always providing subconsciously the environments and the arrangements."

An investigation into the allegations is being conducted by An Olive Branch, an organization that specializes in helping spiritual communities deal with ethical misconduct. At Yoga West, Yogi Bhajan's pictures and sayings have been removed from the walls.

Yoga West

1535 Robertson Blvd, Los Angeles, CA 90035

Guru Ram Das Ashram

1620 Preuss Rd., Los Angeles, CA 90035

INN of the
Seventh
Ray
CREEKSIDE
DINING

INN OF THE SEVENTH RAY

A mainstay of the Topanga Canyon scene since the height of the hippie days, the Inn of the Seventh Ray restaurant opened serving healthy organic fare in 1973. It is rumored to have been built on a sacred site of the Chumash and to have perhaps been a private retreat spot for Aimee Semple McPherson (see page 68). And one of her lovers? We will never know.

The Seven Rays is a concept popularized by Madam Blavatsky and Theosophy (see page 63), sometimes related to the seven chakras, sometimes to seven angelic beings, seven substances that make up the created universe, seven psychological types, and so forth. Each ray has a different occult energy, with the Seventh being the penultimate.

The website talks about the food being:

"energized as a gift from the sun with a dash of esoteric food knowledge and ancient mystery school wisdom tossed in for your seasoning and pleasure ... The food is prepared with the greatest of care and creativity and charged with the vibration of the violet flame of the Seventh Ray for perhaps your personal transportation to a higher plane."

Photo left: Inn of the Seventh Ray

Inn of the Seventh Ray

I've eaten there twice with twenty-five years in between, and both times, the food was fresh, healthy, and tasteless, and both times the service was cheerful, friendly, and incompetent. Maybe it's just my luck, because you can't be a successful business for that long running like that. Maybe people continue to come because the setting is so beautiful – dining outdoors under a canopy creekside "partake[ing] of the angelic vibrations" is a Spiritual L.A. experience not to be missed.

Next door visit the Spiral Staircase, a gift shop jam-packed full of books and trinkets.

Inn of the Seventh Ray

128 Old Topanga Canyon Rd, Topanga, CA 90290

AND A WEALTH OF OTHERS

THE RISE OF THE NEW RELIGIONS

The independent spirits of Californians were more open than most to the metaphysical and inward-focused religions emigrating from the East, both the East Coast of the U.S. and the Eastern Hemisphere. Traditional religions still spoke to the majority of Angelenos, yet a growing number felt a greater affinity with the new religions such as New Thought, Christian Science, Theosophy (see page 63), Religious Science (see page 140), and the loosely-affiliated zeitgeist formerly referred to as "New Age." In time, these sects grew to be more popular here than in their places of origin.

The new religions, however, were primarily middle to upper-middle-class educated white people, and did not necessarily lead to relationships with Latino, African American, Jewish, Native American, or Asian neighbors. Although the new religions speak to being open to all, the reality is that the memberships are highly homogeneous except for a few welcome and popular examples such as Agape International Spiritual Center (see page 158).

New Thought Movement

An umbrella term for a group of religions including Religious Science, Divine Science, Unity Church, and much of the self-help movement. Their beliefs include positive thinking, the law of attraction (first written about in 1906), personal power, creative visualization, that divinity is inside each person, and that our minds create our reality.

Religious Science is actually a Spiritual L.A. hybrid developed by Ernest Holmes, author of *The Science of Mind.*

New Age Movement

Although not really a movement, and not really about the "new age," the number of people considering themselves to be "spiritual but not religious" is one of the fastest-growing trends in American culture. Since the 1970s, what we might term mind-body-spirit has become increasingly visible in the specialized bookstores, yoga studios, crystals, restaurants, magazines, and gift shops (looking surprisingly like high-priced botánicas – see page 29), and audibly in the type of music played for massage and in yoga classes becoming the New Age category for the Grammys.

The spirituality is highly individualistic, with each person's experiences being the source of authority. It is often a mixture of wherever the individual's search has taken them: Eastern religions, the counterculture of the 60s, alternative medicine and holistic health, modern Paganism, Western Esotericism, Carl Jung, UFOs, and the Human Potential Movement. There is generally a belief in divinity, although that definition is again, individual. The central tenet seems to be that each must cultivate one's own divine potential.

Although many might say the epicenter of this movement is Esalen Institute in Northern California, anyone who has spent time in Santa Monica would have to agree: it wears the New Age crown.

Founder's Church of Religios Science

THE SCIENCE OF MIND

Another homegrown L.A. religion is the Church of Religious Science, part of the group of movements known as New Thought (see page 138). Ernest Holmes (1887-1960) moved to Venice, California, in 1912 from the East coast where he had been a student of Mary Baker Eddy, the founder of Christian Science. He gave his first talk downtown at the Metaphysical Library in 1916, kicking off a speaking tour that took him around the nation for the next ten years. He lived in L.A. for the rest of his life.

Dr. Holmes published his book *The Science of Mind* in 1926, and began speaking to large audiences in L.A. at such places as the Biltmore Hotel, the Ebell Theatre, and the Wiltern. In 1954 the Church of Religious Science was incorporated, and it now counts over four hundred congregations and forty thousand members.

The Science of Mind and Dr. Holmes' work has had a huge influence on the self-help movement. It promotes using the power of the mind for healing and fulfillment, controlling one's thoughts, and holding a belief in a desired outcome. Instead of referring to Spirit as God, they call it Universal Mind, and believe in the unity of all life. Part of the offerings at the Church is Spiritual Mind Treatments, or Affirmative Prayer, where a petitioner is aided by a statement of their desired outcome as having already happened. "Amen. And so it is."

Although he eventually broke away to start his own church, Michael Bernard Beckwith and Agape (see page 158) have been heavily influenced by Dr. Holmes and the Church of Religious Science.

Founder's Church of Religious Science

3281 W 6th St, Los Angeles, CA 90020

The Metaphysical Library (now The Brack Shops)

527 W 7th St, Los Angeles, CA 90014

TOUR

MIDTOWN SPIRITUAL L.A.

Photo right: Guru Ram Das Ashram

We don't usually think of Midtown when we think of Spiritual L.A., but it's there, it's there.

1. **Agape International Spiritual Center**
   Currently housed at the Saban Theatre. Check out the charisma, the music, the vibe (see page 158).
   8440 Wilshire Blvd, Beverly Hills, CA 90211

2. **Kabbalah Center**
   Previously movie star central (see page 144).
   1062 S Robertson Blvd, Los Angeles, CA 90035

3. **Yoga West**
   Yogi Bhajan's place with all those white-turbaned people (see page 132).
   1535 S Robertson Blvd, Los Angeles, CA 90035

MIDTOWN SPIRITUAL L.A.

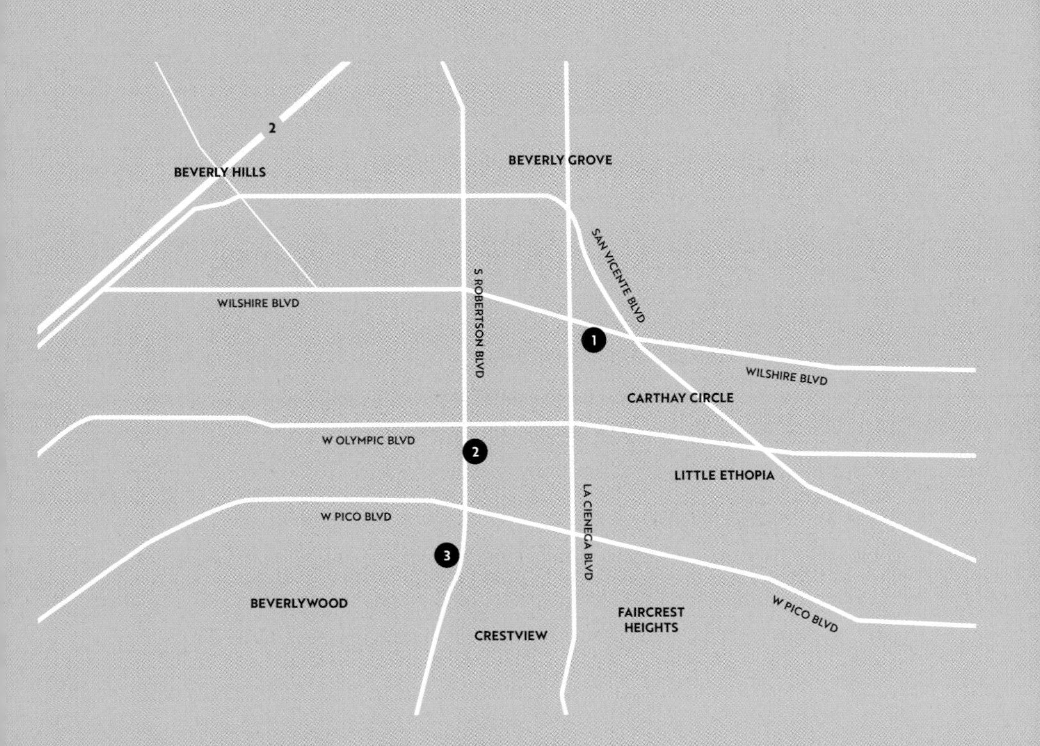

MADONNA AND THE RED STRING BRIGADE

In the early 2000s celebrity gossip (how did we keep up before the Internet?) was rife with news of the latest Kabbalah converts: Madonna, Donna Karan, Britney Spears, Ashton Kutcher and Demi Moore. Sporting a red string around one's left wrist was a sign that you were in on the secret, secrets that were previously available only to learned scholars.

Actually, the only scholars let in on the mystic secrets were Jewish men over the age of forty. When Philip and Karen Berg began their Kabbalah teachings, their goal was to make this ancient wisdom available to everyone without exclusion. As Karen Berg says on her website:

"If wisdom can help improve the lives of others, it should not be kept a secret."

Of course, the idea that spiritual truth should be available to any and all comers has raised controversy whenever it has surfaced through the ages. The Berg's version of Kabbalah has been seen by traditionalists as a perversion of the ancient wisdom tradition and instead, as New Age self-help.

In 1984 the Bergs founded The Kabbalah Centre in L.A. where it begat a worldwide movement. At its height it was reported to have several million followers and over fifty centers worldwide. When Philip died in 2013, Karen Berg and their two sons, David and Yehuda assumed the helm.

Some of the Kabbalah teachings are that a unifying truth underlies all religions, that what we can perceive with our senses comprised only one percent of reality, a strong belief in astrology, and the precept that by one's efforts one can remove blocks in the way of receiving spiritual energy (Light).

Kabbalah Centre offerings include online courses, books, articles, videos, events, livestreams, spiritual travel, and membership in a worldwide community. The instructors' photos as posted are uniformly young and attractive.

Kabbalah Centre

Multiple scandals and lawsuits have plagued the Centre over financial and sexual improprieties. Previous members report being gouged for money in multiple ways, and a charity the Centre co-chaired with Madonna was suspected to be funneling money directly to itself. There were IRS and FBI investigations in 2011, and membership dropped sharply. Yehuda Berg, one of the two sons, paid damages and stepped down. Current estimates are that three thousand to five thousand core members remain.

I was curious about the infamous red string, so I visited the bookstore to check it out. The Kabbalah Red String Pack, a piece of red thread wrapped around a rectangle of cardboard, costing probably a dime (or less) to make in China, retails for twenty-six dollars – perhaps a small price to pay to ward off the Evil Eye. The online version is sold out.

Kabbalah Centre

1062 S Robertson Blvd, Los Angeles, CA 90035

MINDFUL MASTERS

L.A. has almost as many places to meditate as it has one-dollar taco stands, from luscious outdoor gardens (see page 228), to yoga studios, and independent and chain meditation centers. A particular form of meditation called mindfulness focuses the attention on the present moment, without judgment and with calm acceptance. Most mindfulness practices are based in contemporary Buddhism. Because this method is so deceptively simple, many claim to have mastered it after a weekend workshop, but it is an art that yields greater benefits the longer one practices.

Out of L.A.'s plethora of meditation centers, here are two headed by phenomenal women who've been walking their talk for decades, dedicating their lives to spreading mindful awareness.

InsightLA

This growing meditation community offers classes, retreats, events, and a teacher training program with three locations around L.A. Founded twenty years ago by Trudy Goodman, Ph.D., InsightLA was the first center to combine traditional meditation with mindfulness practices such as those popularized by Jon Kabat-Zin. Trudy is InsightLA's lead teacher, a psychotherapist of twenty-five years, a meditator for forty, and she teaches and travels with her husband, best-selling Buddhist author, Jack Kornfield, Ph.D.

- *1430 Olympic Blvd, Santa Monica, Ca 90404*
- *4300 Melrose Ave, Los Angeles, CA 90029*
- *9940 Westwanda Dr, Beverly Hills, Ca 90210*

Mindfulness Awareness Research Center (MARC)

MARC is two-fold: the scientific research center at UCLA, and the public programs. Founded by heavy-hitter authors and scientists, Susan L. Smalley, Ph.D., and Daniel J. Siegel, M.D., MARC has done much to bring mindfulness into the mainstream.

The public programs offer classes, workshops, and the very popular Weekly Drop-in Meditations at the Hammer Museum and online, which are also available as a podcast. These meditations are led by Diana Winston, Director of Mindfulness Education. Diana has been practicing mindfulness since 1989 and teaching since 1993, and is according to the *Los Angeles Times* "one of the nation's best-known teachers of mindfulness." You can experience Diana's teachings anywhere on the free downloadable app *UCLA Mindful*. If you prefer meditating in Spanish, Dr. Eric Lopez-Maya will guide you into deep relaxation.

MARC at UCLA

- *740 Westwood Plaza Room C8-237, Los Angeles, CA 90095*

Hammer Museum

- *10899 Wilshire Blvd, Los Angeles, CA 90024*

ANGEL FACE, ANGEL FOOD

Another of L.A.'s star-shining spiritual rockstars is Marianne Williamson (1952 - present), author of eleven books selling more than three million copies, four of which were *New York Times* bestsellers. Williamson is the spiritual teacher and advisor to many in Hollywood and beyond, not only through her books but also due to her livestream talks that broadcast worldwide.

Certainly, a contributing factor to her success is her angelic good looks, but Marianne Williamson is far from just a pretty face. In 1989, she founded Project Angel Food, a program serving meals-on-wheels to homebound people with AIDS in the L.A. area. Today, the Angel program has expanded to include people with other serious and disabling illnesses and delivers more than ten thousand meals per week.

Williamson began her public career as a popularizer of *The Course in Miracles*, a series of books claiming to be the correct interpretations of Jesus's teachings, channeled with his help. Williamson's appearance on *Oprah* spread the word to millions, and many claim to have been profoundly influenced.

A frequent guest not only on *Oprah*, but also other prominent media outlets such as *Good Morning America and Larry King Live*, Williamson shares her spiritual message widely. Newsweek magazine named her one of the top fifty most influential baby boomers. She has been increasingly moving into the political sphere, stepping up as a Presidential candidate and encouraging other women to run for office.

Marianne Williamson is one of the few spiritual figures I could find no dirt on. It appears she has generated zero controversy or gossip except for having a daughter whose father she refuses to name. Does anyone care about such things anymore? Perhaps Marianne Williamson truly is an angel in human form. Listen to Marianne Williamson's livestream lectures based on *The Courses in Miracles* Monday evenings at 7:30 pm or see her live at The Saban Theatre.

Saban Theatre

8440 Wilshire Blvd, Los Angeles, CA 90211

MAYBE A LITTLE TOO HOT

You've probably heard of hot yoga, maybe even taken a class or two. Not every yogi knows, however, that the originator of the set of twenty-six postures and two breathing exercises done in a room heated to 104 degrees is Bikram Choudhury, currently under investigation for six rape charges. Bikram was previously found guilty of sexual harassment with the victim awarded $6.8 million in punitive damages.

Bikram was born in India in February, 1946, where he studied yoga with Bishnu Ghosh, brother of Paramahansa Yogananda. It is widely reported that at the age of eleven, Bikram was the youngest person to win the National India Yoga Competition, a title that he held for three years. However, research into the matter does not find any evidence of a National India Yoga Competition existing at that time, or at any time for that matter.

Bikram moved to L.A. and began what was to become his yoga empire, at one time consisting of more than seven hundred Bikram Yoga Schools around the world. In 1994, he began his nine-week, twice-yearly teacher trainings which attracted up to four hundred students paying $12,000 each. His wealth, estimated at $75 million, enabled Bikram and his wife and partner, Rajashree, to live a rich, Beverly Hills lifestyle including owning dozens of luxury cars and friendships with Hollywood stars. Bikram is famous for wearing only a black Speedo in class. (What's with the gurus and Speedos? see page 130) For many of his students he was their spiritual leader as well.

Then in 2013, seven women filed sexual assault lawsuits against him. One of them, a lawyer who worked for him, was awarded the above damages but has not been able to collect the money as Bikram escaped to India in 2016 to avoid further prosecution. He claims the charges are untrue.

Bikram tried to trademark his set of poses but was denied, as the judge said it was like Arnold Schwartzenegger trying to copyright bench presses. Bikram has pursued aggressive lawsuits against students who borrow or copy his work.

Because of the scandal, teachers and studios of Bikram's method have begun distancing themselves from him, erasing his name. You'll notice if you visit the Bikram Yoga L.A. website, it doesn't even mention Bikram.

Outside the US, he continues to thrive, promoting his lucrative teacher training camps. Watch *Bikram: Yogi, Guru, Predator* on Netflix for the full scoop.

Peace Awareness Gardens

PEACE AWARENESS LABYRINTH & GARDENS

Billing itself as "A Spiritual Oasis in the City," the Peace Awareness Labyrinth and Gardens is a gift of the Movement of Spiritual Inner Awareness (MSIA) (see page 128). A free meditation garden, there are numerous terraces with places to sit and contemplate, listen to the trickle of water fountains, or walk the labyrinth which is a replica of the one at Chartes Cathedral in France built in 1214.

Admission is free, but you'll need to make a reservation in advance. First-time attendees are required to attend a brief informational tour about the house and property, thankfully without any aroma of proselytizing.

Lots of staff or volunteers were attending to various tasks while I was there, working on computers or doing set-up for that evening's event. I kept getting asked if I was okay, and where was my badge? It was a bit unnerving, but perhaps all this attention to security is due to the fact that the gentrification of the surrounding neighborhood is going slowly.

The Gardens felt confined and overly supervised to me, and I did not get a "spiritual vibe." However, my friend Michael loves it and goes frequently to meditate and get centered. He says he always feels incredibly calm and refreshed after his visits there.

Our tour guide never mentioned Arianna Huffington (see page 154), so I asked if she is still involved. "Oh yes," he said proudly. "She most definitely is."

Peace Awareness Labyrinth

Peace Awareness Labyrinth and Gardens

3500 W Adams Blvd, Los Angeles, CA 90018

Peace Awareness Gardens

ARIANNA HUFFINGTON: SPIRITUAL ADEPT

We all know Arianna Huffington as the larger-than-life media personality: president and co-founder of the *Huffington Post*, best-selling author of fifteen books (her *The Fourth Instinct: The Call of the Soul* states that our drive for spirituality is as great as those for sex, survival, and power), former candidate for Governor of California after years as a politician's wife, and "the Sir Edmund Hillary (the first Caucasian to top Mount Everest) of social climbers" who has amassed an estimated net worth of $315 million.

Arianna's PR machine, however, keeps secret the fact that she occupies a seat very near the top of the hierarchy of MSIA. Arianna has always kept a low profile about it, even publicly denying the degree of her involvement. In a fascinating, well-researched *Vanity Fair* exposé, the author, Maureen Orth, caught her in a number of lies.

These are indisputable facts: In the late 1970s, Arianna was ordained an MSIA minister. She has attained their highest level of secret initiation, "Soul Initiate." She followed John-Roger all over the world for decades until his death, and continues to make large tax-deductible donations to this work she supports.

Ms. Orth writes that Arianna received large "consulting fees" to introduce her high-level friends to John-Roger, and that her marriage to the gay, fabulously wealthy Michael Huffington was part of a master plan to put her on the political map.

Of course, if Arianna Huffington is deeply involved in a spiritual group that gives her sustenance and support, more power to her, and we would wish the same for everyone. As one of my early mentors whispered to me, "The magicians have always worked in secret."

THE SCHOOL IN THE CLOSET

The University of Santa Monica (USM) offers masters degrees, doctorates, and certificates in "spiritual psychology." The website states that the classes "take place in an uplifting Soul-Centered learning environment that nurtures the awakening of the human Spirit inherent in each student... [providing them] with practical information, tools, and experience for transforming their consciousness and transforming their lives." The curriculum emphasizes a "culture of giving."

This might sound wonderful – but why are they hiding the fact that USM was founded by John-Roger and disseminates his teachings? Why is this information buried deep in the fine print on the website? Why is USM not upfront about it? This seems another example of the secrecy perpetrated by MSIA (see page 128), and intended to dupe the public.

Also, the teachings of MSIA is not what I know of as "spiritual psychology." I personally have a master's degree in "spiritual psychology," an all-inclusive term that includes the breadth of Eastern and Western religions, psychologies, Native traditions, psychedelic research, and mysticism – a very different subject of study than the dogma of one man. This seems duplicitous as well.

University of Santa Monica

On the other hand, I've personally met several people who attended USM who give it nothing but glowing reviews. Something good must be going on there because these people were radiating with life force themselves. So, who knows? MSIA, come out of the closet!

University of Santa Monica

2107 Wilshire Blvd, Santa Monica, CA 90403

Agape International Spiritual Center
+ Saban Theatre

WE LET, WE LET IT BE

If you've never been to a service at the Agape International Spiritual Center, you ought to go if just for the music. Or the sense of joyous celebration, or for the fact that your neighbor will greet you with loving-kindness. Services are definitely a finely crafted show: the entertainment value is enormous.

Agape was founded and is headed by the charismatic Michael Bernard Beckwith, author of several books including *Life Visioning* and *Spiritual Liberation*. You may have seen him in one of his frequent media appearances on shows such as *Dr. Oz*, *Oprah*, *The Secret* (which wasn't really a secret, now was it?), or his own PBS special.

Founded in 1986, Agape grew to prominence with the partnership of musical director, Rickie Byers, who for many years was Rickie Byers Beckwith. At the time of this writing the Beckwiths are involved in what appears to be a contentious divorce.

Agape is a proponent of New Thought (see page 138) spirituality. It has an active educational component in its weekly classes and in its University of Transformational Studies. There is a large outreach emphasis in its various ministries, such as to the bereaved, elderly, LGBT, youth and families, and other volunteer opportunities.

During a service one can feel the spirit of *agape*, the Greek word for unconditional love. With nine thousand members and up to a million attending on livestream, attendees are a strikingly attractive, well-dressed, intelligent group of people of cultural and racial diversity. (Single people have been known to attend for the hopeful planned or "cute meet.")

What are you doing this Sunday? If you haven't been, why not? Agape is one of the mainstays of Spiritual LA. You will be treated to Michael Beckwith's message of hope and love and to a joyous choir singing the songs of Rickie Byers. If you go at 11:00 a.m., there's also an interpreter who dances and sings for the deaf community. Services currently held at the Saban Theatre.

Agape International Spiritual Center + Saban Theatre

8440 Wilshire Blvd, Beverly Hills, CA 90211

International Society for Krishna Consciousness of Los Angeles

HARE KRISHNA HARE KRISHNA

You could go just for the food and the people watching. The restaurant is full of attractive vegetarian foodies savoring the inexpensive, all-you-can-eat, fresh, tasty colorful food, that just-by-the-way is *prasad* (has been blessed).

Or, you could go just for the boutique upstairs full of magical, spiritual treasures: *saris* and *kurtas*, jewelry, statues of gods and goddesses, ayurvedic products, *malas*, and books. Prices are reasonable making it quite difficult to leave without finding some new article of clothing or a *tchotchke* you can't live without.

Many people are put off by the idea of visiting the Hare Krishna Temple, imagining they'll be trapped by orange-clad geeks sporting strange hairdos, but really, it's not like that. A few of the devotees may dress unusually, but they're not any weirder than someone you'd see at a skate park. The ones I've met are polite and quiet, and there is zero proselytizing going on.

The Los Angeles temple was the first world headquarters of The International Society for Krishna Consciousness (ISKCON), founded in 1966 by their Guru, Swami Prabhupada. Their core beliefs are based on Hindu scriptures and tend to be rather fundamentalist in practice. They believe in *bhakti* yoga, which is a spiritual path focused on the cultivation of love and devotion toward God. ISKCON today is a worldwide organization with more than five hundred and fifty centers.

If you do want to visit the Temple, which many people never do, you'll find a silent sanctuary inside. If they're having a service, you'll observe a Hindu ritual of worshipping divine statues led by a monk singing Sanskrit chants, blowing a conch shell, and waving incense.

Over the years, many celebrities have been involved with the Hare Krishnas including the Beatles, Steve Jobs, Allen Ginsberg, Poly Styrene of X-Ray Spex, and Russell Brand, who married Katy Perry in a Hare Krishna ceremony.

Over the years, the Krishnas have also been involved in numerous scandals which are easy to research on the Internet: racketeering, mail fraud, stockpiling guns, potential murder, and the physical, emotional, and sexual abuse of children. While certainly not great you have to ask yourself, is it any worse than the Catholic Church?

The temple hosts the Festival of Chariots every summer, a fantastic event where the Krishnas take over a large stretch of Venice Beach and provide music, various booths, and free food to up to twenty thousand people. You read that right: twenty thousand. One of the Krishna missions is to feed the hungry and they serve up to two million free meals every day in sixty countries.

International Society for Krishna Consciousness of Los Angeles

When you visit, you won't even have to hear the chant *Hare Krishna* if you'd prefer not, but on the other hand, why wouldn't you want to? The Krishnas believe that listening to the Hare Krishna mantra promotes "peace, happiness, God-realization, freedom from repeated birth and death, and total self-fulfillment." Hey, personally I'll take whatever help I can get.

International Society for Krishna Consciousness of Los Angeles

3764 Watseka Ave, Los Angeles, CA 90034

WESTSIDE GURU

Turns out you don't have to travel to India to meet a guru – one's available right here in L.A. The concept of a guru is misunderstood in the West, but to many people worldwide it means help from someone more evolved than oneself. Many gurus' devotees belong to a sangha, the community of spiritual seekers surrounding him or her, and say that the combined energy radically accelerates their transformation. You know, if you're okay being an average tennis player and rallying with your friends, you don't need a coach, but if you aim for the big leagues ... the same may be true in spiritual life.

Swami Premodaya's devout followers here and in L.A. will attest to his help in their lives spiritually and personally. Premodaya worked for over thirty years as a therapist and psychiatric administrator before he became a guru, so he has profound knowledge of the psychological as well as the spiritual. He has a graduate degree in Transpersonal (spiritual) Psychology and is a lifetime devotee of Osho. To add to Premodaya's intense life experience, he was born in a refugee camp after WWII, and his parents were in the concentration camps.

International Centers of Divine Awakening (ICODA) was founded in 2004 by Bodhisattva Shree Swami Premodaya in Los Angeles. The main headquarters is in L.A. with another in Brussels. ICODA offers online and in-person satsangs, discourses, workshops, retreats, community gatherings, private sessions with Premodaya, and Life Management sessions with Prem Prasad, Premodaya's charismatic son who also serves as ICODA's Spiritual Director.

Even if having a guru is not your thing, Premodaya's kind and gentle nature and stand-up-comic wit may tickle your funny bone and bring you peace and understanding.

International Centers of Divine Awakening (ICODA)
Check out their website at ***icoda.org***

TELEPATHIC INSTRUCTION FROM THE MASTERS

Another hometown Spiritual L.A. sect is the Christian/Theosophical hybrid, Niscience (pronounced nish-ence). Founded in in Glendale in 1953 by the charismatic Ann Ree Colton (1898 - 1984) and her twenty-four-year-younger husband, Jonathan Murro, Niscience is a blend of Eastern and Western thought.

Colton developed a system for personal and spiritual growth in a series of twenty-three books based on telepathic instructions, psychology, dream analysis, Christianity, and Eastern religions. This system of lessons is still available as a home-study course. At the Glendale location visitors can listen to recordings of Ann's teachings on ESP, reincarnation, and past lives.

Ann Ree Colton Foundation of Niscience

During the height of Nicience's popularity, several hundred members would gather most nights at the Glendale compound for spiritual talks, fasting, prayer, and worship. Colton's reported warmth attracted great devotion among her followers, something that her husband, after her death in 1984, was unable to sustain.

Jonathan Murro committed suicide in 1991 after allegations that he had embezzled money (although investigations found no evidence) and that Niscience was an oppressive cult. He was unable to maintain the level of enthusiasm Colton had inspired in her followers. The organization is still strong today.

Ann Ree Colton Foundation of Niscience

336 W Colorado St, Glendale, CA 91204

SPIRITUAL HIPSTERS

Yoga Heaven

Just driving around L.A. one would surely assume we have more yoga studios per capita than anywhere else, but no, that crown goes to ... ready? Alaska! Believe it or not, California only ranks sixth among the most yoga-obsessed states. Nevertheless, L.A. has a plethora of yoga studios offering classes of all persuasions, from the gentlest and most relaxing to the athletically extreme. L.A. yoga teachers often reach movie-star status.

Yoga first began in L.A. with the arrival of Yogananda in 1925, followed by Indra Devi opening the first yoga studio in Hollywood on the Sunset Strip in the late 1940s. B.K.S. Iyengar Yoga Institute came to L.A. from India in 1984 and is still holding classes today. Yoga Works birthed in Santa Monica in 1987 and has since expanded to a national chain including twenty-three studios in Southern California.

Check out a full list of L.A.'s current and popular yoga studios online or on an app such as Mindbody.

Devi Yoga Institute (no longer there)

8806 Sunset Blvd, West Hollywood 90069

Original Yoga Works

2215 Main St, Santa Monica, CA 90405

Kirtan Paradise

Almost as popular as yoga in this city (and often to the same people) is kirtan – the group singing of mantras as call-and-response. This repeating the names of god is believed to raise the consciousness of listeners, and indeed, one can get quite high and happy listening and singing along.

Traditional kirtan has been going on at the Hare Krishna Temple in Culver City since the 70s. Contemporary Western kirtan, however, had its beginnings in the

Yoga Works

90s with Krishna Das, Wah!, Jai Uttal, and our home town hero, Dave Stringer. In 2009 the now-defunct Bhakti Yoga Shala opened, and the hipster kirtan scene evolved spreading out to yoga studios, private homes, and festivals here and across the world.

To find kirtan happenings, check events calendars, yoga studios listings, and Meetup.com. You can also plan to attend the two local "Coachellas of Kirtan" – Bhakti Fest, held in the fall, and Shakti Fest, in the spring.

VENICE AND SPIRITUAL L.A.

Venice Beach has long attracted artists and writers, the counterculture, and spiritual seekers of all kinds. Enjoy the bohemian vibe while it lasts, as Venice is rapidly gentrifying due to the arrival of Google and Snapchat. Here are some examples of Spiritual L.A. in Venice:

- The Beat Generation (Beatniks) explored Zen Buddhism among other paths and frequented the Venice West Café on Dudley and the Gas House on Ocean Front Walk in the 50s.
- Jim Morrison, lead singer of The Doors, considered by many a rock shaman channeling spiritual energy, lived in Venice for two years.
- Aimee Semple McPherson's controversial disappearance (see page 68) occurred here when she walked into the water at Venice Beach.
- Most days you can walk along the Boardwalk and receive a reading from one of the many tarot card readers, astrologers, and so on.

Venice Beach Boardwalk

- The annual Festival of the Chariots is held here in August during which time the Hare Krishnas feed thousands of people for free.

- The Mystic Journey Bookstore offers talks, workshops and readers.

- Full Circle Venice was a spiritual community that focused on millennials and their search for individual enlightenment and group consciousness, an updated version of their parents' New Age. Former teen-heartthrob, actor Andrew Keegan, and his crew attracted stylish young people and the Burning Man crowd. The schedule of events included workshops, group meditations, music, and classes. Full Circle offered weekly Activ888 ceremony on Sundays at 10 am until they closed in 2018.

- The astrology chart of Venice has a Grand Trine in water and Sun conjunct Neptune in Cancer.

DAY TRIPS

TOUR

DESERT DAY TRIP

First, call or email ahead and book a Sound Bath at the Integratron. The time of your session will determine how to route your itinerary for the day. This trip may warrant an overnight stay – you'll not want to miss any of these fascinating, mysterious locations of greater Spiritual L.A. history:

1. **Integratron**
   A hippy, trippy, domed time machine (see page 176).
   By appointment only.
   2477 Belfield Blvd, Landers, CA 92285

2. **Giant Rock**
   No longer accessible unless you have a four-wheel drive.
   Do you? (see page 180)
   Giant Rock, CA 92285

3. **Joshua Tree Retreat Center and Institute of Mentalphysics**
   Vortex central (see page 186)
   59700 Twentynine Palms Hwy, Joshua Tree, CA 92252

Pappy & Harriet's

4 Desert Christ Park – Yucca Valley

A kitsch classic. (see page 188)

56200 Sunnyslope Dr, Yucca Valley, CA 92284

5 Joshua Tree Inn

Center of the Universe for the 1970s desert spiritual explosion (see page 182). Many famous rock stars of the 60s lived and partied here. Room 8 is where Gram Parsons, highly influential country rock musician, died and the room is rumored to be haunted.

61259 Twentynine Palms Hwy, Joshua Tree, CA 92252

DESERT DAY TRIP

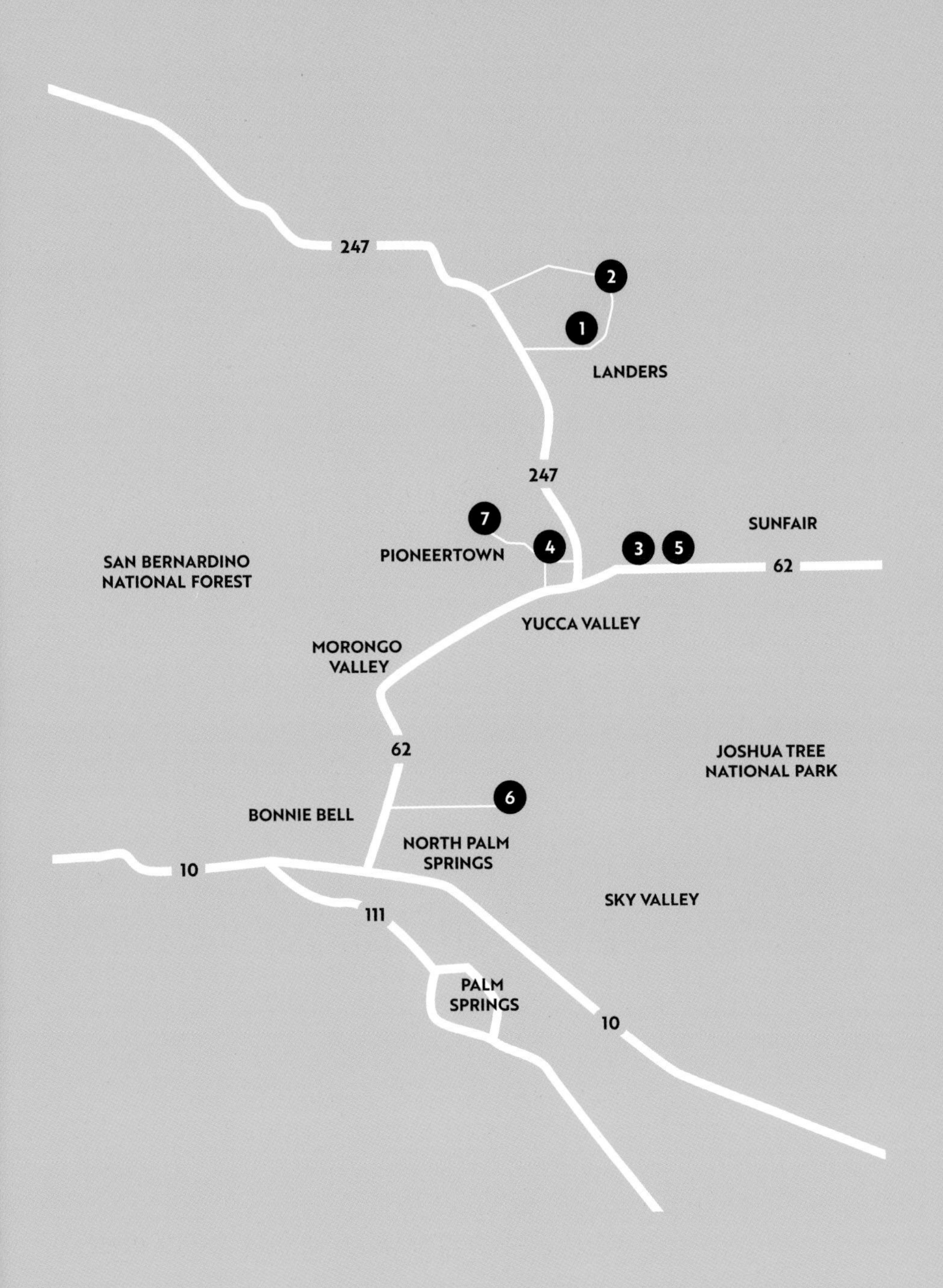

6 Cabot's Pueblo Museum

One man's compound where he hosted the local Theosophists (see page 190).

67616 E Desert View Ave, Desert Hot Springs, CA 92240

7 Pappy and Harriet's

While not particularly spiritual per se, Pappy and Harriet's is an in-the-know destination for a meal and/or drink due to, well, mostly due to the fact that it is out in the middle of nowhere. Impress your friends.

53688 Pioneertown Rd, Pioneertown, CA 92268

Desert Hot Springs

Also, before you return to L.A., stop in for a relaxing soak at one of the many natural hot springs. The indigenous Cahuilla considered the springs to be sources of sacred power and used them for healing ceremonies. Perhaps you can create a healing ceremony of your own.

Pick a spot before you go – available at all price points and poshness or lack thereof.

WEIRD SCENES INSIDE THE GOLDMINE

The above lyric from The Doors song "The End" does not even begin to describe the varieties of spiritual-seeking that have gone on in Joshua Tree and the surrounding desert since the beginning of recorded time.

First of all, the land itself is riddled with vortexes and ley lines attesting to strong spiritual energy (see page 36).

Secondly, the land around Giant Rock and the Integratron was holy land for the Native Peoples where the northern and southern tribes met annually.

Third, Joshua trees were named by Mormon travelers who imagined a desert filled with praying plants – to them the trees looked like the prophet, Joshua, holding up his arms to God in supplication.

There are more reported UFO sightings in Joshua Tree and the Mojave Desert than any other place in the U.S. In the 50s this brought an influx of the curious, the eccentric, and the rich. (Whether this has anything to do with spirituality is debatable, but to many, it does.)

In addition to the spiritual flowering in the 50s, there was another in the 70s concerning spirituality, hallucinogens, rock 'n' roll, and the counterculture. The above-cited Jim Morrison of The Doors often took acid trips in the area, as did The Rolling Stones, Donovan, and many musicians to follow. John Lennon recorded *The Joshua Tree Tapes* in the 70s.

Of course, U2 later recorded their album, *The Joshua Tree*. And among a certain crowd, partaking of drugs in the desert remains a popular pastime.

All in all, however you plan to enjoy it, you are in store for a magical time on a day-trip tour of the desert.

STOP
Please
SOUND BATH
IN PROGRESS

THE INTEGRATRON

A hippy, trippy, domed time machine constructed in the 1950s to promote longevity and interplanetary communication. The Integratron was built at the intersection of geomagnetic energy lines, designed with explicit instruction from ETs from Venus (which included building the wooden structure entirely without nails), and financed largely by Howard Hughes.

If that isn't enough to warrant a visit, inside the dome is an acoustically-perfect rotunda where the public can reserve Sound Bath sessions: Tibetan bowls are played, and the sound resounding in the dome produces a profound state of relaxation, which it is said, is healing.

The Integratron had fallen into disrepair until 2000, when it was purchased by the Karl sisters. Under their stewardship, it has been cleaned up, opened to the public, began offering Sound Baths, and is now available for event rentals. Think of it: you could lease it for a private party, invite your favorite DJ, all your friends, and rave to the full moon. Musicians of all types also come to record in the perfect acoustics.

Be sure to book ahead. If you show up at the gate without a reservation, you won't be allowed to enter no matter how charming you are.

The Integratron

2477 Belfield Blvd, Landers, CA 92285

Photo left: The Integratron

THE INTERPLANETARY AIRPORT AND THE COME ON INN

One of the more unconventional individuals in Greater L.A. spiritual history was George Van Tassel (1910 - 1978). Van, as he was called, used knowledge he received from ETs to build the Integratron and held yearly UFO conventions at Giant Rock that attracted upward of eleven thousand attendees.

Van Tassel had worked in the aerospace industry before moving himself and his family to Giant Rock in 1947 to take over the tiny airport landing field there. They lived in the hollowed-out rooms under the rock, and Mrs. Van Tassel started a small café called The Come On Inn.

In 1953, Van was visited by a ship from Venus that took him aboard and taught him the secrets of life extension, time travel, and metaphysics. He continued over the years to receive transmissions from a being named Solgonda, which led Van to write several books including *I Rode a Flying Saucer*. Van Tassel started The Ministry of Universal Wisdom to share the information he was receiving.

The family ran UFO conventions at Giant Rock from 1953-1978 featuring all the big names from the time: scientists, UFO contactees, and meditators who attended the sessions in Van's home under the Rock. The money generated from these gatherings was used to help build the Integratron.

George Van Tassel died unexpectedly in 1978 at the early age of sixty-eight. The family compound at Giant Rock was left to ruin and was eventually bulldozed by the Bureau of Land Management. Interestingly, the FBI kept files on George Van Tassel, which to this date have not been released.

GIANT ROCK

Giant Rock was a sacred spot for Native Americans who referred to it as the "Great Stone" because as the largest object in the area, it symbolized the Great Spirit. Neighboring tribes gathered there yearly, with only the chiefs and elders allowed close to the holy rock. The rest of the tribes camped a mile away. The rock is said to be at a major crossing point of the Earth's ley lines.

To George Van Tassel (see page 178), this largest free-standing boulder in the world was sacred in another way, for it was here that he claimed to have been contacted by ETs from Venus who took him aboard their ship and taught him to build the Integratron. For years he and his family lived in a home hollowed out underneath the Rock, ran the Interplanetary Airport and the Come On Inn, and held yearly UFO Conventions with up to eleven thousand attendees.

After Van Tassel's death in 1978, the buildings fell into disrepair and were finally bulldozed. In 2000, the Giant Rock split into two pieces which some believed to be foretold as a sign of the millennium.

Today it's not possible to visit Giant Rock unless you have a four-wheel drive, and even then, the trip is reportedly hell on your vehicle. Perhaps it's worth it? Some of us will never know.

Giant Rock, CA 92285

JOSHUA TREE NATIONAL PARK

People not on a spiritual quest go to Joshua Tree National Park for the hiking, nature trails, strange landscapes, and the wildflowers, and JT is a big rock climbing destination. It is definitely awe-inspiringly beautiful, and there are many sporting opportunities.

Spiritual people, however, have been long attracted to the region for these and other reasons: the "energy," the ley lines and vortexes, the unearthly silence that naturally leads to a quiet mind and meditation, the attraction of UFOs and nature spirits. Many questing types go to the Park to take psychedelic drugs to help reach higher states of consciousness.

I couldn't locate where the mountain is where all the rock stars went in the 60s (see page 182) other than to learn that it is twelve miles in. After numerous internet searches, I left two voicemails for the Park Service that were unreturned. They don't want people to know about this? They don't want the Park used this way? That's a shame – we'd like to check it out.

There are two entrances to the Park: one on Highway 10 beyond Palm Springs, and the one in 29 Palms off Highway 62 which makes more sense for this Tour.

Joshua Tree Visitor Center

6554 Park Boulevard, Joshua Tree, CA 92256

ROCK STARS, PEYOTE, AND THE VOICE OF AN ETHEREAL BEING

The Rolling Stones *et* entourage traveled to the high desert mountain to await UFOs with him. He directed the video of Timothy Leary's wedding on the mountain where the presiding shaman was too stoned on acid to perform the ceremony. The infamous campfire scene in *Easy Rider* in which Jack Nicholson riffs on UFOs and the "Venusian invasion" is rumored to have actually taken place at one of Ted Markland's psychedelic field trips to the desert mountain in Joshua Tree.

Besides his career as a charismatic friend to the curious and the famous, Ted Markland (born 1933) was an actor on many of the hit TV shows of the 60s, working steadily until his death in 2011 at the age of seventy-eight.

Markland had been an attendee at one of George Van Tassel's (see page 178) annual UFO conventions at Giant Rock. In an interview he stated that the first time he visited the mountain, he had been fasting and heard "the voice of an ethereal being," saw a rainbow, and experienced a profound spiritual awakening. Afterward he made frequent weekend trips to the mountain, bringing with him celebrities including the above-mentioned rock stars, Dennis Hopper, Peter Fonda, and Steve McQueen.

When the Stones visited Markland's mountain along with Marianne Faithful and Anita Pallenberg, Mick compared the energy to Stonehenge and other Druid sites he'd visited. A famous photo shoot taken by Michael Cooper of Keith Richards, Gram Parsons, and Anita Pallenberg at the height of the psychedelic rock era in 1969, shows them all in their youthful, ethereal beauty amidst the stark desert landscape.

One of the celebrities Markland took to the desert was Gram Parsons, an influential musician who some say invented the genre of country rock. Gram died at age twenty-six in 1973 of an overdose at the Joshua Tree Inn. His room 8 has been enshrined, and fans still hold vigil every year on September 19th.

In 1975 Markland relocated to the desert permanently and raised a family. The legend lives on. Rockstars continued the pilgrimage to the desert including U2, Victoria Williams, John Lennon (who recorded the rare *Joshua Tree Tapes* there), Jim Morrison, and a rockstar of a different vein, Anthony Bourdain. The folk-rock troubadour Donovan said, "Somewhere out in that far distant landscape there's a secret mountain where there was a door to another world."

Joshua Tree National Park

West Entrance, Junction of Hwy 62 and Park Blvd at Joshua Tree Village

Joshua Tree Inn

61259 Twentynine Palms Hwy, Joshua Tree, CA 92252

Author's Note:

The best I could come up with from my research was that this stuff happened "twelve miles into the park." We drove into Joshua Tree National Park, measuring carefully twelve miles from the entrance on Highway 62. At mile twelve the energy changed drastically. Suddenly there were cars, day hikers, children, families, loud music -- tourists everywhere visiting the Hall of Horrors (a group of striking rock formations) and Saddle Rocks climbing areas.

We stopped the car, got quiet, tuned in and listened closely, attempting to locate the place where those previous psychonauts had explored alternative spirituality. One of us would get a strong hunch it was over there, then the other of us, over there. We each have our strong suspicions which hill it was, but no proof. Somewhere in Joshua Tree is the mystical mountain, lost in today's sanitized theme park world. Maybe you'll be the one to find it? Please let me know when you do.

Joshua Tree Inn

Joshua Tree Retreat Center

JOSHUA TREE RETREAT CENTER AND THE INSTITUTE OF MENTALPHYSICS

Where can you go to explore vortex energy yourself? The Joshua Tree Retreat Center (JTRC) claims to have eighteen vortexes on its 420-acre property. Download a map or stop in at the bookstore to find out where to check them out.

JTRC, the first and the largest retreat center in the West, hosts numerous events throughout the year including the well-attended Bhaktifest and Shaktifest, Holotropic Breathwork retreats, and workshops by New Age Superstars such as Byron Katie, Jack Kornfield, Deva Premal and Miten, and so on.

In addition to the vortexes, the property includes gorgeous desert landscapes, native plants, a labyrinth, medicine wheel, swimming pool and warm pool. Frank Lloyd Wright (himself a student of the spiritual teacher, George Gurdjieff) and his son Lloyd designed the buildings according to principles of sacred geometry. You might be lucky enough to spot a bunny or a roadrunner while strolling the grounds.

JTRC offers many choices of accommodations including camping. If you are one of the people (like me) who find the atmosphere a bit rustic, there are a plethora of choices of hotels and Airbnbs from Yucca Valley to 29 Palms.

The Institute of Mentalphysics was founded L.A .in 1928 by Edwin J Dingle (1881 - 1972), a rumored-to-be reincarnated Tibetan monk. Dingle was one of the first Westerners to study in Tibet, and he synthesized his learnings into his own work which has been studied by 220,000 students and is now available as a correspondence course and during retreats on the land. Mentalphysics is a blend of breathing exercises, meditation, and "universal laws that, if followed, are believed to lead to mastery of oneself and all of Life."

Dingle moved the Institute to Yucca Valley in 1941 to what is now the Joshua Tree Retreat Center.

The Institute of Mentalphysics

59700 Twentynine Palms Hwy, Joshua Tree, CA 92252

DESERT CHRIST PARK

In a residential neighborhood overlooking the desert town of Yucca Valley lays Desert Christ Park, where ten dilapidated Biblical scenes sculpted in plaster stand in various states of disarray. The visitor can faintly identify the Sermon on the Mount, but with the other scenes, it is difficult to tell what they depict. A giant bas-relief of the Last Supper stands untouched.

When artist Antone Martin (1887-1961) retired from Douglas Aircraft in 1951, he started building a three-ton statue of Jesus in the driveway of his Inglewood home. The plan had been for Jesus to be placed at the rim of the Grand Canyon, but Antone was denied a permit. Instead, on Easter Sunday, 1951, the statue was installed on the hillside overlooking Yucca Valley.

Working alone for the next ten years, Antone created his sculptures in concrete, then covered them in plaster and white paint. He was able to finish the project before he died. Thankfully, he did not live to see his grand work destroyed by earthquake damage and vandalism.

Desert Christ Park

The creation of yet another dreamer with a unique spiritual vision, Desert Christ Park emanates with the love Antone Martin poured into it. You can feel the pathos on the faces of some of the remaining statues, and it is delightful to breathe in the aura of these strange desert visionaries and their eccentric expressions of love. Funds are being collected to restore the park, but – (pray that I don't bring down the Wrath of God by saying this) – I hope they don't. It's pretty darn cool the way it is.

Desert Christ Park

56200 Sunnyslope Dr, Yucca Valley, CA 92284

DESERT HOT SPRINGS - CABOT YERXA

Another fantastical desert dreamer was Cabot Yerxa (1884 – 1965) who when he found hot springs on his land in what is now Desert Hot Springs, built a compound that you can now visit as a museum.

Yerxa was quite the multi-faceted character: architect, artist, writer, builder, adventurer, visionary, entrepreneur, and activist for Native American rights. His home design was inspired by Hopi Indian pueblos and consisted of a trading post, an art gallery, his workshop, and the family's living quarters.

Cabot's Pueblo Museum

Cabot Yerxa 's former home

Cabot is of interest to Spiritual L.A. because he was a highly-degreed Mason and the founder and president of the Theosophical Society in Desert Hot Springs. He and his wife Portia Graham held theosophical and metaphysical classes in their home.

If you visit, much of the grounds can be toured for free. There is a twenty-minute video that will tell you more than you probably want to know about Mr. Cabot, although it includes no mention of his spiritual leanings. His image has been cleaned up for public consumption – although we here at Spiritual L.A. know who he was.

Cabot's Pueblo Museum

67616 E Desert View Ave, Desert Hot Springs, CA 92240

TOUR

SPIRITUAL L.A. DAY TRIP EAST

There are two international Zen Centers on a day-trip east: one in Idyllwild and one on Mount Baldy (the one where Leonard Cohen lived).

1 Yoko-ji-Zen Mountain Center

Visit on a Sunday when they offer a beginner's Zen Meditation Instruction class at 9:30 a.m. (Coffee and tea are available from 8:30 a.m.) Afterward there is a dharma talk followed by a vegetarian lunch. When I went everyone was quite friendly and the food was simple but delicious.

58900 Apple Canyon Rd, Mountain Center, CA 92561

2 Mount Baldy Zen Center

Not really open for visitors, you can rent rooms or take retreats there. The abbot presided over the center until his death at age 102. Songwriter Leonard Cohen lived there on and off.

7901 Mt Baldy Rd, Mt Baldy, CA 91759

Mount Baldy

With or without visiting the Zen Center, Mount Baldy is not to be missed (see page 194).

❸ Hsi Lai Temple

The largest Buddhist temple in the West, located on over fifteen acres. There are massive gold statues of three Buddhas who achieved enlightenment: Shakyamuni (the historical Buddha), Amitabha (Limitless Light), and Bhaisajyaguru (healing). Parking is free. Very busy on the weekends.

3456 Glenmark Dr, Hacienda Heights, CA 91745

❹ Salvation Mountain

"I just want to prove to the people that God is love."

Leonard Knight's masterpiece (see page 195)

Beal Rd, Calipatria, CA 92233

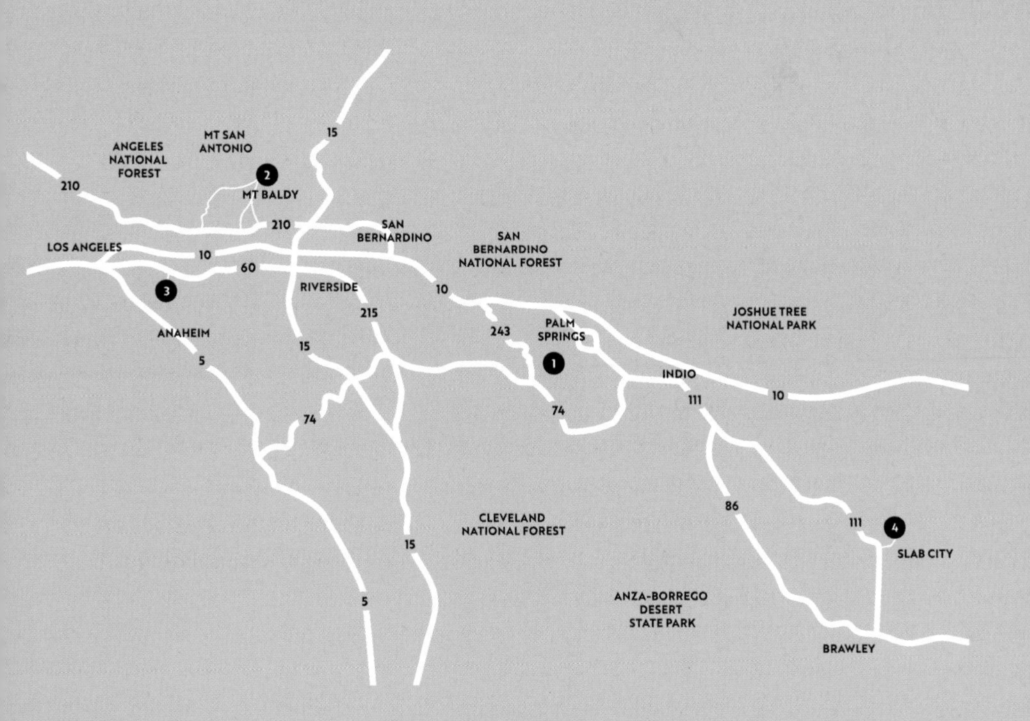

SACRED MOUNT BALDY

Mountains everywhere have inspired spiritual feelings -- in the face of vast vistas, the ego becomes right-sized. Whether we're in a car or standing still after hiking with all our endorphins pumping, the view from the summit is exhilarating. We can't deny that we're not running the show, that something grander is going on. New Agers have compiled lists of holy mountains on the planet, including designating certain mountains as chakra centers of the earth.

Mount Baldy has a particular history of holiness. The highest peak in Los Angeles County, it was revered as a sacred mountain by the Tongva Nation, and young braves were sent there on vision quests. The Mount Baldy Zen Center, made famous by the singer/songwriter Leonard Cohen's residence there, has been on the mountain since 1971. George King, the founder of the Aetherius Society (page xxx), channeled energy on the mountain and stated, "The energies of Mount Baldy help the pilgrims to have a deeper cosmic appreciation." The Society conducts monthly hikes and holds its annual World Peace Pilgrimage there.

Mount Baldy is about an hour outside L.A, depending on traffic. You'll find a rickety, old ski lift leading up to a restaurant and bar. Please be forewarned that the altitude of 8,600 feet is not for everyone – altitude sickness is common between 6,000 and 8,000 feet and may cause nausea, dizziness, and headaches. If that doesn't afflict you and yours, Mount Baldy is a lovely place to hike, and who knows? ... maybe meet some extraterrestrials.

Salvation Mountain

A FRENZY OF LOVE

Three hours from L.A., way out beyond Palm Springs and the Salton Sea, lays Salvation Mountain, one man's spiritual gift to the world. Proclaimed by Senator Barbara Boxer as a national treasure, this "mountain" is covered in multi-colored paint and proclaims the message that God is Love.

For twenty-five years Leonard Knight (1931–2014) poured his heart, soul, and over one hundred thousand gallons of paint onto the hill he built of adobe and straw. Salvation Mountain is covered with Biblical verses and Christian sayings and contains special rooms and alcoves filled with decorative art. If you wish to climb to the top, signs will point out the Yellow Brick Road to lead you up. The other visitors when I was there were assorted hipsters and Goth kids, apparently folk art aficionados. A newly-married couple from China were having photos taken in their gown and tux.

During a spiritual awakening at age thirty-six, Leonard realized that the answer to life was not complicated: just accept Jesus Christ, repent, and love everybody.

GOD
IS
LOVE
THE HOLY BIBLE
YOU ARE LOVED GOD
GODS HOLY BIBLE
SAY JESUS I'M
A SINNER PLEASE
COME UPON MY
BODY AND INTO
MY HEART
JOY
PEACE
GENTLENESS
LONG SUFFERING
KEEP OUT

LO
VE
IS
UNIVERSAL
LOVE
GOD
IS
LOVE

He spent several years attempting to spread the word to organized religion which rejected his message as too simplistic. Leonard moved to Niland in 1984 and began working full-time on his masterpiece, living in his truck even when temperatures hit the one hundreds.

Salvation Mountain was featured in the 2007 film *Into the Wild*. A photo of Coldplay atop the Mountain appeared on their *A Head Full Of Dreams* album.

Visiting Salvation Mountain

I'm not sure if the six-hour round trip would be worth your time. The videos on YouTube are so excellent that might be enough. If I weren't writing this book, they probably would have sufficed, the actual site being almost anticlimactic after the great filmmaking of the videos.

However, the drive out included unexpected delights: Highway 78 winds alongside the Salton Sea, an eerie, dead, inland body of water that looks as I imagine Loch Ness does and stinks to high heaven from the rotting fish. There are picturesque abandoned restaurants and compounds covered in graffiti from the days it was a real resort, with many intriguing photo ops.

The town of Niland is a rare treasure for an urbanite. You'll witness a slice of life you'd never see in L.A.: people renting space in an RV park for $400 a month amid the deserted, defaced buildings, enduring the Salton Sea stench, bragging with their Trump stickers; the whole town looking like it's been bombed out. It certainly opened my eyes to people whose lives I hadn't known about.

And on the other hand, if you don't go, you'll miss experiencing Leonard Knight's passion in person. There is something mesmerizing and humbling about a man with such single focus using his life to spread the message of Love. Either to watch on YouTube or to be there personally at Salvation Mountain is to stand in awe of his frenzy of love.

Beal Rd, Niland, CA 92257

Photos on previous page + right:
Salvation Mountain

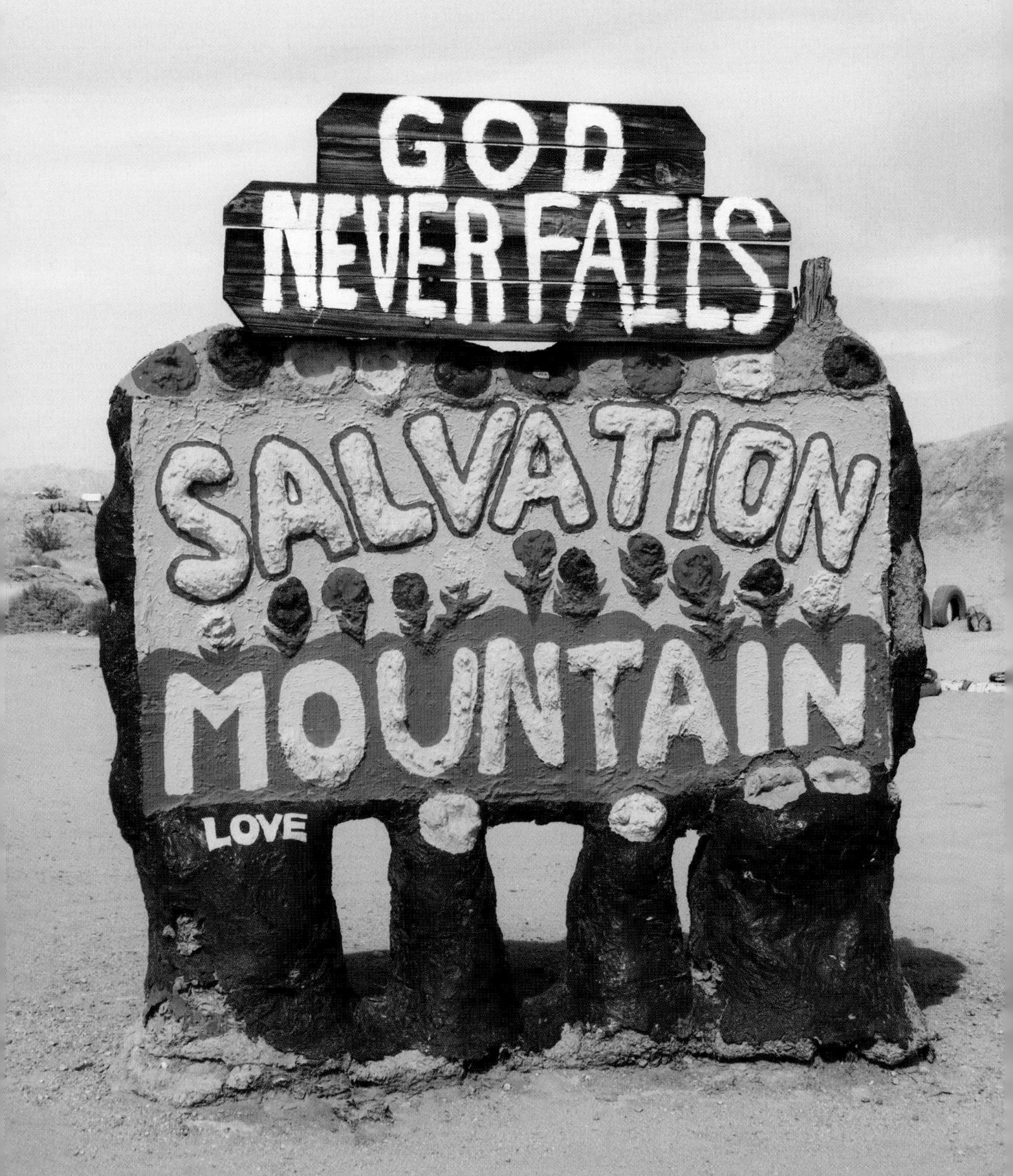
GOD
NEVER FAILS
SALVATION
MOUNTAIN
LOVE

TOUR

DAY TRIP SANTA BARBARA

On your way up the 101, while passing through Thousand Oaks stop and check out the:

1 Chumash Cultural Center

On the site of a former Chumash village named Sap'wi. Wonderful museum, a replica of a Chumash village, and pictographs.

3290 Lang Ranch Pkwy, Thousand Oaks, CA 91362

2 Old Mission Santa Barbara

We'd heard that the Mission is a strong spiritual vortex and decided to check it out. It seemed unlikely considering the usual violence and genocide perpetrated by the Catholic friars against the Native Peoples. However, when onsite we were bowled over by the powerful spiritual energy, especially radiating from the altar. Definitely worth the trip. We also brought home holy water captured into tiny bottles purchased in the gift shop.

2201 Laguna St, Santa Barbara, CA 93105

Photo right: Old Mission Santa Barbara

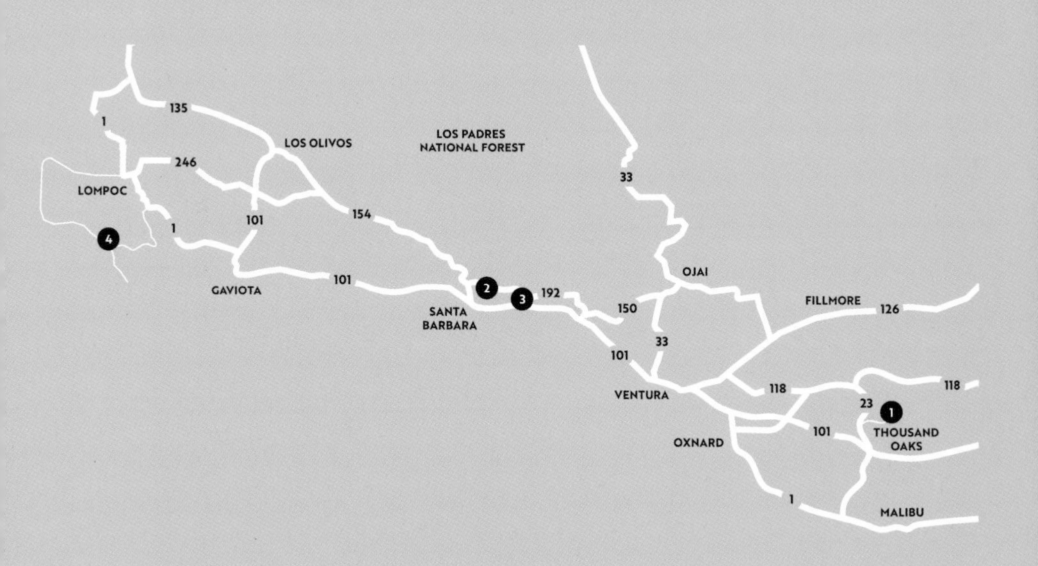

3 **Shalawa Meadow**

Ancient Chumash burial site. Strong shakti. Public parking at the end of the street. Walk through the flowering lane, turn right at the beach, and walk until you see the Meadow on your right. (see page 204)

Eucalyptus Lane, Santa Barbara 93108

4 **The Western Gate**

If you dare (see page 206).

Jalama Beach County Park

9999 Jalama Rd, Lompoc, CA 93436

Photo left: Hammond Trail,
Santa Barbara

SHALAWA

SHALAWA MEADOW

A location that was sacred to the Chumash and radiates considerable shakti is the Shalawa Meadow in Santa Barbara. Shalawa (also called Hammond's Meadow) was an ancient burial site and ceremonial place. This whole coastal region is and has been extremely significant to Native Americans due to its proximity to the Western Gate.

A monument at the Shalawa Meadow has colorful ceramic tiles adorned with animals along with this inscription: "The Sacredness of the land lies in the minds of its people. This land is dedicated to the Spirit and memory of the ancestors and their children."

We nearly missed the Hammond Trail because it was unmarked. It turned out to be a long, narrow, flower-filled tunnel on the right side of the parking lot which was enchanting to walk down, as if fairy tale creatures might appear at any moment. After the short walk and a crossover on a bridge we arrived at a beach full of surfers, dogs, and happy families picnicking. After a bit more, on the right amid McMansions we saw a rough "meadow" full of gopher holes and weeds. The monument is visible from the beach, or we might have missed it.

The meadow is a bit dilapidated; the monument is chipped and broken, but the power of the place is unmistakable. We felt moved to circumambulate the area, stopping frequently to say prayers. Energy radiated out more strongly in some areas than others, but overall, we experienced an enhanced aura of radiance and reverence.

Of course, white developers have fought contentious battles with the Chumash over the Meadow. A movement was begun in 1979 to protect the sacred nature of the site, and the Chumash were joined by surfers and some of the residents. Today, plans are being made for a possible ceremonial garden and the planting of native plants. I was happy to hear that the planning meetings finally include input from the Chumash.

Shalawa Meadow

Eucalyptus Ln, Santa Barbara 93108

Photo left: Shalawa Meadow

THE WESTERN GATE

When I heard there was a portal for souls passing through to the other world north of Santa Barbara, I had to go. The Western Gate (Humquaq) is a sacred place for the Chumash – a gateway where the dead enter the heavens on their way to paradise (Similaqsa). I trust one hundred percent that when Native people identify a place as sacred, it will be a powerful energy vortex.

The Western Gate sticks out as the farthest point west on the Western Hemisphere, and is the natural divide between Northern and Southern California. The location is so important to the Chumash that they identify themselves as "The Keepers of the Western Gate." At the eastern-most point of the continent on Long Island, NY, is Montauk, the Eastern Gate.

Chumash souls went to what is now called Point Conception and ascended to the Milky Way. As the soul entered the gate of heaven, it is said that a loud noise was heard. The entire one-hundred-square mile area is sacred and mysterious: There are rumors of Chumash ruins under the water below the Point, where the sea is teeming with schools of dolphins, seals, sea lions, whales, and sharks, all communing together.

Turns out it's not so easy to get to. At the time I heard about it, the Western Gate was a private ranch, fenced off so you couldn't get there by car. The closest you can drive is Jalama County Beach, so I drove the almost three hours it takes to get there, parked, and walked the ten-mile round-trip on the beach toward the lighthouse at Point Conception.

On the drive up, I fantasized about this place with so much sacred power, this portal to another dimension. Were the people who owned it ignorant of its identity? Were they black magicians harnessing the power for personal and/or nefarious use? What if the landowners were instead powerful white magicians, working their juju at the farthest west point of the Western Hemisphere, performing rituals to keep the world turning?

The area has long been a battleground with developers as have many locations once belonging to the Native people. Over the years the land has been owned or fought over by Spanish and Mexican ranchers, real estate developers, gas and oil companies, and of course, someone who wanted to build a golf course. The federal government confiscated the furthermost tip and built the lighthouse in 1856. In 1978, hundreds of Chumash and their supporters staged a year-long occupancy to prevent the building of a natural gas facility. (They were successful.) In 2007, the land was bought by a hedge fund, which was really scary, but when real estate prices nose-dived in the 2008 crash, they sold it and got out.

Turns out I was right – the land is controlled today by powerful white magicians doing good things with their money and the metaphysical power of the Western Gate. In 2017, Jack and Laura Dangermond, tech billionaires, bought the land for $225 million and donated it to the Nature Conservancy to be permanently protected. Their mission as a couple is to encourage other one-percent-ers to leave their wealth to conservation efforts. When I watched their interview on YouTube I realized, this is what angels look like: baby boomer gazillionaires – who knew? The stewardship of the Nature Conservancy may be a step toward eventually creating public access to Point Conception and thus, to the Western Gate.

Personally, I had strange, inexplicable, metaphysical experiences at the Western Gate. I considered sharing them with you, but that's for another book. Suffice it to say, the Western Gate is without a doubt a portal to another reality. I'm cautious about going back, but I will. Maybe you and I will see each other on the trail: burn some sage, leave some tobacco, and say a prayer for all.

Jalama Beach County Park

9999 Jalama Rd, Lompoc, CA 93436

Krishnamurti Library

Meditation Mount

Krotona Institute of Theosophy

Krotona Bookshop

TOUR

DAY TRIP TO OJAI

Most day-trippers to Ojai (pronounced oh-high) don't identify as being on a spiritual quest, though nearly everyone will contend there's something about the vibe. The restaurants, wineries, spas, charming Airbnbs, and quiet hiking trails are enough reason to drive an hour and a half north of L.A. to get away for a few hours. Many artists, hippies, rich people, and celebrities have settled permanently. But conventional people are missing learning about Ojai's rich spiritual history, and what it is that makes up that special energy.

The Chumash Indians originally considered the Ojai Valley to have healing properties, nourished by the plentiful natural hot springs. The non-Indian identification of Ojai as a spiritual place began in 1878 in an article in the *L.A. Times* that called it "the magnetic center of the earth... where people come to reach the God centers in themselves." In the 1920s, a magazine article by a Dr. Hrdlicka stated that a "sub-race of superior humans" was being born and to house them, Annie Besant of the Theosophists (see page 63) bought 465 acres in Ojai. She then brought Krishnamurti, "the new Messiah," to live there, and Theosophists from all over the world started considering California the "Atlantis of the West."

In 1926, the Krotona Institute (see page 60) moved from Hollywood to Ojai, setting up a compound on over one hundred acres. In 1968, Florence Garrigue, a student of Theosophy, founded Meditation Mount. Since then, life in the Valley has flourished led by the spiritual aspirants and disciples of these alternative religions.

Many in the know consider Ojai to be a spiritual vortex, a power spot, a sacred place; that it possesses magical healing powers, and that it is "a section of Southern California thoroughly impregnated with occult and psychic influences." How about you, do you feel it?

Check out these Ojai spiritual centers:

1 Krishnamurti Library & Study Center

A place to learn about Jiddhu Krishnamurti (1895–1986), the guru who was groomed to be the Theosophist world teacher but when he came of age, rejected the title and the responsibilities. Instead, he became a spiritual teacher in his own right. Inside the Library you'll find information on his teachings as well as staff to answer your questions. Be sure not to miss the pepper tree outside under which Krishnamurti experienced his enlightenment.

1130 McAndrew Rd, Ojai, CA 93023

2 Krotona Institute of Theosophy

Krotona Institute of Theosophy welcomes visitors to explore its beautiful grounds, Library and Research Center, Quest bookstore, a labyrinth, the Sanctuary of Connections, and to attend its seasonal programs. An appealing place to meditate, sit in the gardens, and soak in all that mysterious history.

46 Krotona Hill, Ojai, CA 93023

3 Meditation Mount

Florence Garrigue created this meditation garden and House when she was eighty years old, and she ran it clear up until two years before her death at ninety-eight. She had had a lifelong mission to create meditation programs to benefit the world, and when she found this property, created the future she wanted to see.

The lovely gardens overlook the Ojai Valley, and it is utterly inviting to relax on one of the benches, listen to the birds sing, or stroll along the walking path. The mind falls easily into silence here.

The Meditation House is mystical and empty, with crystals and sacred symbols of various world religions. Formal meditations are held here each morning and on Full Moons. Note that the door is hand-carved with signs of the zodiac.

10340 Reeves Rd, Ojai, CA 93023

Ojai Wineries

Why not? If you're looking for "spirits" of another kind, many wineries and wine tours dot the Ojai area. After all, Jesus was a wine drinker ...

Various locations, Google yourself a wine map

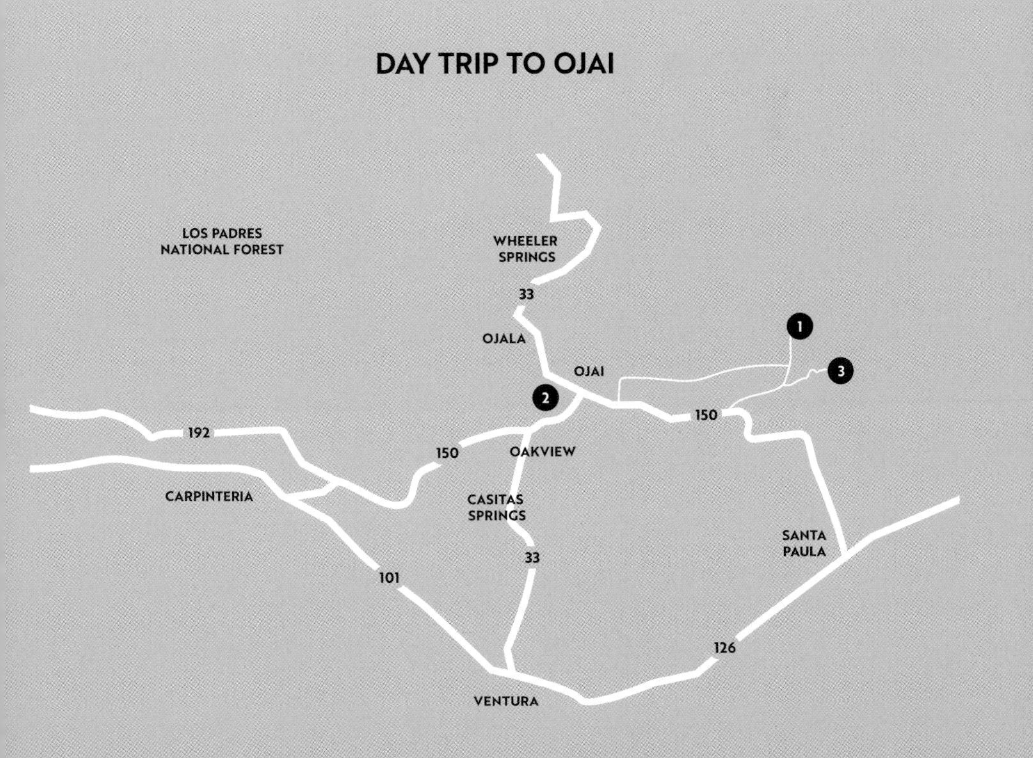

TOUR

DAY TRIP SOUTH

Start early to visit the Glass Church before any weddings are scheduled, as later it can be impossible to get in. Enjoy a leisurely drive down the Coast to SRF Encinitas and eat lunch at Swami's. Stop and experience Puvunga on your way back. If you're concluding the day at Glen Ivy, be sure to book ahead.

Wayfarers Chapel aka "The Glass Church"

Designed by Lloyd Wright (not Frank Lloyd Wright, but his son) and built in 1951, the Wayfarers Chapel is not to be missed. It is a beautiful place for expansive heart-opening meditations. Even the drive in is breathtaking, as the Chapel is built high on a bluff overlooking the Pacific.

The Chapel Interior is built mostly of glass, and also stone, wood, and foliage. Outside are gardens and panoramic views of the ocean. For one dollar you can buy a pamphlet to a self-guided tour of the property: the Front Lawn, Reflection Pool, the Tower, the Rose Garden, Meditation Garden, Visitors Center and Gift Shop. Be sure and stop for all the vistas along the way.

The Wayfarers Chapel was built as a memorial for Emanuel Swedenborg, the eighteenth-century theologian and mystic. The religion and church he founded, the Swedenborg Church, has about three thousand adherents worldwide.

Photo left + next page:
Wayfarer's Chapel

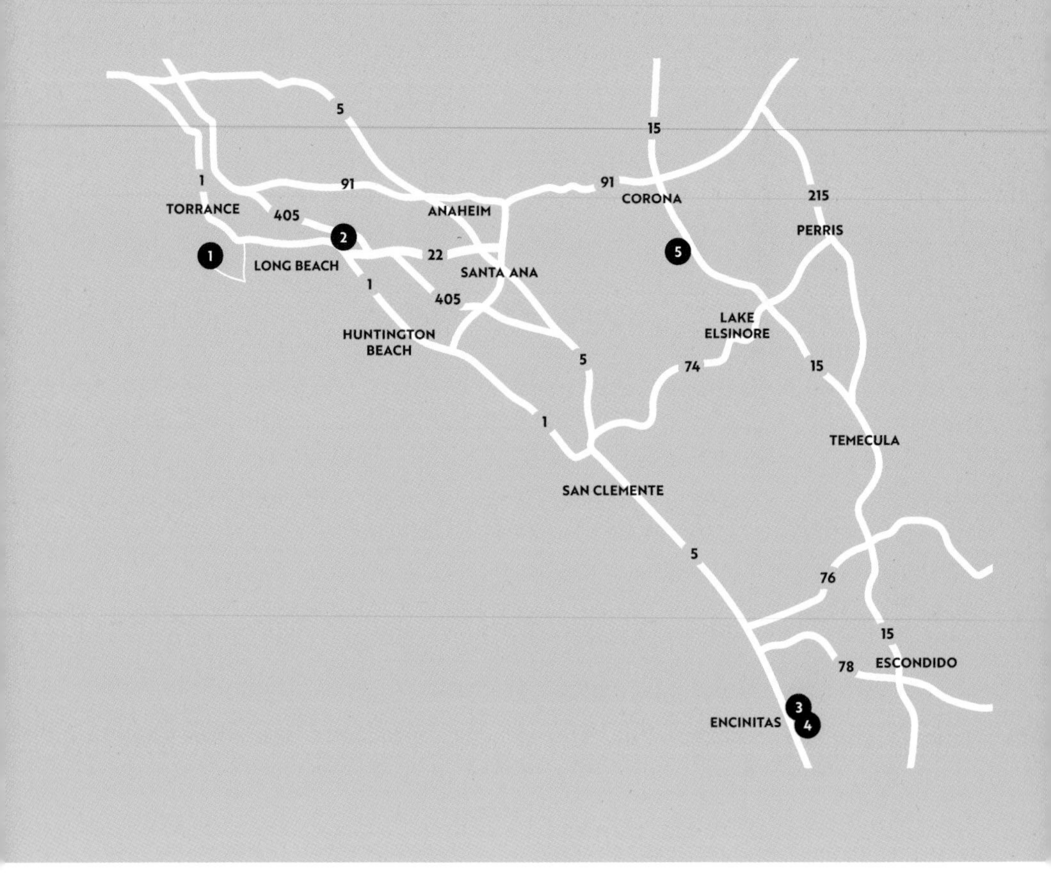

Some of the major tenets of the faith are the interconnection of all of life, the further awareness of the new age in which we live, respect for all viewpoints, and the belief that God is infinitely loving.

5755 Palos Verdes Dr S, Rancho Palos Verdes, CA 90275

2 Puvunga

Where the Tungva believe the world began (see page 20). On the grounds of Cal State Long Beach. Follow the signs to the Earl Miller Japanese Garden. Park and walk behind the Garden to a clearing with totem poles.

1250 Bellflower Blvd, Long Beach, CA 90840

Photos left + right: Self-Realization fellowship, Encinitas

❸ Self-Realization Fellowship – Encinitas Temple

Paramahansa Yogananda's reach spread down the Southland (see page 46) as far as Encinitas. You're welcome to leisurely stroll the meditation gardens with panoramic views of the Pacific, attend service in the temple, and visit the gift shop. Definitely worth the drive, this place never fails to put one in the state in which all is right with the world.

939 2nd St, Encinitas, CA 92024

❹ Swami's Café

When you visit the SRF Temple, it is almost a requirement that you eat at Swami's, located just across PCH. Although it appears to be a hippie hangout, they serve a full menu. Be sure to not miss the mural of a surfing Yogananda on the kitchen wall.

1163 S Coast Hwy, Encinitas, CA, United States

❺ Glen Ivy Hot Springs

Although today Glen Ivy is a mainstream day spa hosting up to twelve hundred guests on weekends, until it was sold to developers in 2014 it was the undercover home of the spiritual group Emissaries of Divine Light who used it as a healing center. Guests were welcome to use the red-clay mud baths, but it was much more a spiritual retreat than it is today. You may or may not want to pay the rather steep admission price to attend, but it is fun to know about this tiny slice of Spiritual L.A. history.

25000 Glen Ivy Rd, Corona, CA 92883

Swami's Cafe Patio

Mural of surfing Yogananda,
Swami's Cafe

ODDS, ENDS, & ECCENTRICITIES

THE MISS VELMA CHRISTMAS SHOW

"Of course, you can't forget Miss Velma," Greg says. He grew up in the South Bay and remembers watching the annual Christmas pageant on TV. An IMDB search bestows one out of five stars on the show and provides this synopsis: "You can't quite imagine the level of kitsch until you watch the YouTube videos; well, you can't actually watch, but you can fast forward through."

Indeed. On YouTube Miss Velma appears dressed like a doll atop a birthday cake. She arrives onstage seated in a pumpkin, and on the back of a fake white horse. As I fast forward through, she descends out of the sky riding in a spaceship, and preaches from an eagle. There is a celebration of the fifty states, Miss Velma boogying a tribal dance, and a sharp-shooting display. The longer I watch the more jaw-dropping it becomes.

Later we find out that Miss Velma has masterminded the entire show: playing the piano and singing, preaching with great gusto, making all the costumes, utilizing the most up-to-date resources of the time: strobe lights, vocal echo boxes, holograms. Always there is over-the-top showmanship, extravaganza, and surprise.

Velma "Miss Velma" Jaggers (1919 - 2004) and her husband (and cousin) O. Lee Jaggers were among the early televangelists in L. A., along with Aimee Semple McPherson (see page 68). By the mid 60s they were creating their outrageous services at their Universal World Church which continued for decades. The Miss Velma show was televised hundreds of times and was seen in seventy countries. The two believed they had discovered the secrets to physical immortality, but of course they died like everyone else.

As bad-taste as it all may appear to us, we can thank the outsider art community for helping us realize that Miss Velma was endlessly creative in numerous genres, constantly, tirelessly. Frank Zappa, the 70s avant-garde musician and anarchist, was a big fan. Ron Athey, the queer S&M performance artist, wrote an article for *L.A. Weekly* in which he stated that he had been introduced to Miss Velma through his grandmother, and together they'd visited the church again and again. Of Miss Velma he wrote, "She was a healer and an entertainer – saving your soul by capturing your imagination." Through the eyes of these artists we can see that Miss Velma belongs to a unique group of religious art eccentrics along with Leonard Knight of Salvation Mountain (see page 195) and Antone Martin of Desert Christ Park (see page 188).

Visit the Miss Velma Fan Page on Facebook, and check her out on YouTube.

The former site of the Universal World Church

123 N Lake St, Los Angeles, CA 90026

SPIRITUAL L.A. YEARLY CALENDAR OF EVENTS

In addition to traditional religious holidays, Spiritual L.A. celebrates the following. For exact dates, check Facebook or other Events Calendars:

SPRING

- Annual Chumash Day Powwow at Malibu Bluff Park, two days, free to all

- Blessing of the Animals – the Saturday before Easter Sunday on Olvera Street

- The Sunrise Passion Play Service at Vasquez Rocks, Easter morning or the afternoon before, a fully-enacted story of the crucifixion

- Shaktifest – (kirtan festival) Memorial Day Weekend in Joshua Tree

SUMMER

- Summer Solstice Ceremony at Wishtoyo Chumash Foundation

FALL

- World Peace Pilgrimage to Mount Baldy – held in the fall

- The Festival of the Chariots at Venice Beach (Hare Krishna parade), first Sunday in August, forty thousand participants, upward of twenty thousand are fed free meals

- Bhaktifest – (kirtan festival) Labor Day Weekend in Joshua Tree

- Dia de Los Muertos – Mexican celebration "Day of the Dead," around Halloween

WINTER

- Winter Solstice Ceremony at Wishtoyo Chumash Foundation

BEST SPIRITUAL L.A. MOVIES

Including TV shows and videos. In no particular order – watch them all and decide:

Holy Hell – Sex and scandal abound in this film about the Buddhafield cult surrounding the charismatic teacher, Michel. But wait, isn't there something about his eyes?

The Source Family – Fascinating film about the cult surrounding Father Yod and his thirteen wives brings the viewer the full flavor of the spiritual renaissance of the 70s.

City of Angels – Maybe not the best movie in the world, but to see Santa Monica Beach graced by an army of gorgeous angels is worth the price of admission.

Bikram: Yogi, Guru, Predator – Arrogance run amok.

Awake: The Life of Yogananda – Gorgeous.

Children of God (narrated by Helen Mirren) – About the cult that spawned Flirty Fishing.

Reza Aslan's show *Believer* – CNN TV series. The episode featuring Scientology is the only objective, non-hysterical reporting I've encountered.

Strange Angel – CBS TV series on the life of Jack Parsons (with guest appearances by "L Ron Hubbard" and "Aleister Crowley").

6 Generations – Documentary about Chumash history, narrated by a Chumash Elder.

Honorable Mentions – YouTube Docs:

Leonard Knight and his Technicolor Mountain (Salvation Mountain)
Aimee Semple McPherson – American Masters
Joshua Tree – A Planet of Music and Cosmic Energy (psychedelic rock 'n' roll)

TEN PLACES TO GET A READING RIGHT NOW

Going crazy wondering if "S/he loves me; s/he loves me not?" Gain insight into the situation by booking one of the talented readers at these Spiritual L.A. locations. Depending on the time of day, walk-ins or online consults may be available, but it's always best to call ahead.

Alexandria II Bookstore

170 S Lake Ave #100, Pasadena, CA 91101

Phone: (626) 792-7885

The Green Man

5712 Lankershim Blvd, North Hollywood, CA 91601

Phone: (818) 985-2010

House of Intuition

2237 W Sunset Blvd, Silver Lake/Echo Park, 90026

7449 Melrose Ave, West Hollywood, CA 90046

5108 York Blvd, Highland Park, 90042

Phone for all locations: 213-413-8300

Liberate Emporium

1765 Hillhurst Ave, Los Angeles, CA 90027

Phone: (323) 663-6000

Mostly Angels

2602 S Robertson Blvd, Los Angeles, 90034

Phone: (424) 298-8192

Mystic Journey

1624 Abbot Kinney Blvd, Venice, CA 90291

Phone: (310) 399-7070

Psychic Eye

13435 Ventura Blvd, Sherman Oaks, CA 91423

Phone: (818) 906-8263

Venice Beach Boardwalk – various readers daily

Weekends after around 10:00 a.m.

SPIRITUAL L.A. / NEW AGE / OCCULT BOOKSTORES AND SHOPS

Alexandria II Bookstore

Books, tarot cards, magical supplies. Offers psychic readings.

170 S Lake Ave #100, Pasadena, CA 91101

Aum and Garden

Lovely store in the Valley full of gifts and supplies with a full schedule of classes, events, and readings.

13363 Ventura Blvd, Sherman Oaks, CA 91423

The Green Man

Mostly Wiccan supplies. Offers readings.

5712 Lankershim Blvd, North Hollywood, CA 91601

House of Intuition

Three locations carrying books, crystals and stones, magical implements. Offers readings.

2237 W Sunset Blvd, Silver Lake/Echo Park, 90026

7449 Melrose Ave, West Hollywood, CA 90046

5108 York Blvd, Highland Park, 90042

Liberate Emporium

Books, cards, gifts. Offers readings and healing sessions with a variety of practitioners.

1765 Hillhurst Ave, Los Angeles, CA 90027

Mostly Angels L.A.

Tiny, beautiful shop selling crystals, gifts and readings in a neighborhood you wouldn't expect. The shop has recently been taken over by Julian Sambrano – stop in and say hi!

2602 S Robertson Blvd, Los Angeles, CA 90034
1946 Vedanta Pl, Los Angeles, CA 90068

Mystic Journey

Books, incense, gifts, natural healing products. Offers readings, classes, and book events.

1624 Abbot Kinney Blvd, Venice, CA 90291

Open Eye Crystals

Mid-city metaphysical shop featuring crystals, readings, and events.

6110 West Pico Blvd, Los Angeles, CA 90035

Psychic Eye

Books, music, metaphysical supplies, and readings.

13435 Ventura Blvd, Sherman Oaks, CA 91423

Spellbound Sky

Charming shop of "metaphysical notions and potions," full selection of crystals. The owners know their stuff.

4210 Santa Monica Blvd, Los Angeles, CA 90029

Thunderbolt Spiritual Books

Books new and used, gifts, more Eastern in flavor than the occult –oriented stores. The store has a rich history: Carlos Castaneda used to hold classes upstairs.

512 Santa Monica Blvd, Santa Monica, CA 90401

Vedanta Bookstore, Hollywood

Spiritual bookstore focusing on the religions of India. Other traditions are carried as well, although be forewarned, the author's previous book, *Shortcuts to Mindfulness*, was rejected as being "too unconventional."

1946 Vedanta Pl, Los Angeles, CA 90068

SPIRITUAL L.A.'S BEST MEDITATION GARDENS

Ahh ... a moment of silence, a moment to center inside. L.A. hosts countless garden oases (some say living in L.A. means living in a garden itself), but these treasures were designed specifically for meditation:

Hollywood Temple SRF

A quiet oasis in the midst of Hollywood.

4860 Sunset Blvd, Los Angeles, CA 90027

The Lake Shrine

If you haven't been yet, go! One of L.A.'s hidden gems.

17190 Sunset Blvd, Pacific Palisades, CA 90272

Meditation Garden, Cathedral of Our Lady of the Angels

A quiet circular pool for meditation hidden behind the main square.

555 W Temple St, Los Angeles, CA 90012

Mount Washington SRF

Beautiful views overlooking downtown, the Temple of Leaves, the Wishing Well.

3880 San Rafael Ave, Los Angeles, CA 90065

Peace Awareness Labyrinth and Gardens

A garden to enjoy, a labyrinth to walk. It's free, but reservations required.

3500 W Adams Blvd, Los Angeles, CA 90018

Serra Retreat Center Gardens

Serra Retreat Center Gardens

Stunning views of the Pacific and the hillside gardens, relax among the statues of the Stations of the Cross.
Open weekdays.

3402 Serra Rd, Malibu, CA 90265

Wayfarers Chapel

While not technically in L.A., it's worth the drive for a meditative retreat in the garden overlooking the Pacific ocean.

5755 Palos Verdes Dr S, Rancho Palos Verdes, CA 90275

Zen Garden at the Huntington

The entire grounds of the Huntington are potential meditative spots, but the Zen Garden was specifically designed to induce a meditative state. Admission is steep so plan to make a day of it and take in some of the exquisite art while you're there.

Huntington Library, Art Collections & Botanical Gardens
1151 Oxford Rd, San Marino, CA 91108

BEST PLACES IN L.A. TO FEEL THE SHAKTI

It's pouring out ... do you feel it?

- Vedanta Temple (see page 54)
- Yogananda's crypt at Forest Lawn (see page 47)
- Agape (see page 158)
- Bonnie Brae House (see page 72)
- Lake Shrine (see page 49)
- Wishing Well at SRF Headquarters (see page 46)
- Monastery of the Angels (see page 58)
- Our Lady Queen of the Angels church (see page 99)
- Thunderbolt Books (see page 227)

Special Mention (outside of L.A.):

- Old Mission Santa Barbara (see page 200)

Photo right: Old Mission Santa Barbara

TEN SOUTHERN CALIFORNIA VORTEXES

These areas have been identified by vortex experts as either "energy vortexes" – sites of magnified spiritual energy, or places with increased UFO sightings, as noted.

- **Catalina Island**
  Reported UFO activity. (A company states that it gives tours of UFO sightings on the island, but after numerous attempts, I realized no one returns your inquiries.)

- **Desert Hot Springs**
  Energy vortex (see page 190).

- **Fort Tejon (the Grapevine)**
  Paranormal activity.

- **Giant Rock**
  Energy vortex and UFO activity (see page 180).

- **Hollywood**
  Energy vortex (see page 35).

- **Joshua Tree**
  Energy vortex and UFO activity (see page 186).

- **Ojai**
  Energy vortex. Many spiritual organizations make their home there (see page 208).

- **Pyramid Lake**
  Energy vortex.

Zaca Lake

- **Old Mission Santa Barbara**
  Strong spiritual energy pouring out of the altar.

- **Zaca Lake**
  Energy vortex, possible UFO activity.

Footnote:
Zaca Lake was sacred to the Chumash for thousands of years – they believed the lake has no bottom, and the Elders went there to die. In between the Chumash and the current owners, Zaca Lake was owned by a mysterious Human Potential Foundation who pressured the White House to change its policy on UFOs. Today, Zaca Lake is privately owned by a religious organization and is no longer available to the public.

We drove up to Zaca Lake to see if we could visit and found ourselves facing a locked gate with a No Trespassing sign. As we stopped long enough to snap a photo, out of nowhere an ominous, black four-wheel drive with tinted windows drove up behind and intimidated us to leave, which we did. Sometimes I wonder – what if we'd had the courage to say hello? Would we have seen the Men in Black? Aliens? Rednecks? And now I see that the website for the "religious organization" that was up when I began my research has been taken down.

TOP TEN SPIRITUAL L.A. SCANDALS

1. **The Church of Scientology**
   'Nuff said.

2. **Bikram Choudhury**
   Yoga predator gone wild (see page 150 or better yet, watch the movie *Bikram: Yogi, Guru, Predator*).

3. **Aimee Semple McPherson's disappearance**
   She faked her own death! Reported it on her own media empire! (see page 68)

4. **The Babalon Working**
   Jack Parsons together with L. Ron Hubbard performing a black magic rite to usher in the New Age.

5. **Jack Parsons, in general**
   He created JPL labs while practicing occult rituals and writing occult books (see page 84).

6. **Carlos Castaneda**
   Accused of fraud and that his entire work is fictional, all while living with three women (see page 121).

7. **John-Roger of MSIA**
   Various media exposés of mind control, sexual coercion of male followers, and financial wrongdoing. His second-in-command, Peter McWilliams sued MSIA and published *Life 102: What to Do When Your Guru Sues You*.

8. How Manly Hall died

Murdered by his live-in caretaker? Who then took over PRS? His wife thought so. Official records say he died in his sleep, but his body was found in suspicious circumstances. – (see page 66)

9. Swami Kriyananda and Ananda

Thrown out of Yogananda's organization for violating their copyrights and brought to court for sexual abuse, lost the case and was fined $1 million.

10. Ongoing Revelation of Sexual Violations:

- Yogananda – accused of fathering a "love child," (DNA tests cleared him).
- Yogi Bhajan – 16 women have come forward to date (see page 132)
- Noah Levine, charismatic founder of Against the Stream meditation and recovery centers, accused of sexual harassment by several women, kicked out of his own organization
- Zen Center masters accused of sexual harassment for decades at Mount Baldy and downtown
- Pedophile priests in the Catholic Church

TOP TEN SPIRITUAL L.A. BADASS WOMEN

1. **Toypurina**

   Organized and led her people on an attack against the white invaders even though they were vastly outnumbered – doesn't get more badass than that (see page 22).

2. **Aimee Semple McPherson**

   The first media-star evangelist, started her own religion which is still going strong, faked her own death, ran off to Mexico with her lover (see page 68).

3. **Cameron**

   Made art her way, was the occult Scarlet Woman (see page 88).

4. **Marianne Williamson**

   Prominent spiritual teacher at a time it was all men (see page 148).

5. **Zsusanna Budapest** (see page 124)

   Jailed for being a "witch" in the 70s, no, not the 1770s, the 1970s.

6. **Edith Maida Lessing**
   Started her own "love cult," need we say more? (see page 74).

7. **The Flirty Fishers**
   They f*cked for God (see page 114).

8. **Miss Velma Jaggers**
   Bad taste? She didn't and still doesn't care (see page 220).

9. **Ann Ree Colton**
   Started her own religion with her twenty-four-year younger husband (see page 164).

10. **The nuns at the Monastery of the Angels**
    24/7, one of them is on their knees praying for us (see page 58).

TOP TEN SPIRITUAL L.A. ROCKSTARS

Rockstars: Glamorous, charismatic, and sexually magnetic. Moving about the world with a freedom the rest of us envy; all doors are open to them. They incite massive desire, are media sensations, and command the world stage. Whew! These L.A. icons (listed alphabetically) wear the rockstar mantle with royal swagger:

Aimee Semple McPherson

Sexy, hot, rumored to be caught in a love nest with her lover, up to 15,000 people a day came to hear and watch her speak, genius-level use of the media, faked her own death. (see page 68)

Aldous Huxley

Author, handsome, psychonaut, the center of a glamorous international set of intelligentsia: writers, artists, intellectuals, spiritual seekers. (see page 56)

Carlos Casteneda

Lived with three women all reported to be his lovers, refused to be photographed or do interviews which only added to his mystique, worldwide sensation. On the cover of Time magazine in 1973, claimed to move between worlds disembodied. (see page 121)

Cameron

Brave, beautiful, sexy, and drug-addicted, the occultist Marjorie Cameron starred in her own one-woman show at the Museum of Contemporary Art (MOCA) 20 years after her death. (see page 88)

Jack Parsons

Movie-star handsome, rocket scientist, one of the founders of the NASA Jet Propulsion Laboratory (JPL) in Pasadena, rumored to have blown himself up during an occult ritual. (see page 84)

L. Ron Hubbard

Created a world-wide religion from scratch, commanded his own fleet of ships, pursued by the FBI and CIA. (see page 42)

Marianne Williamson

Author of best-selling books, conventional good looks, ran for governor, writes also about sex and spirituality, *Newsweek* magazine named her one of the most influential baby boomers. (see page 148)

Michael Bernard Beckwith

Bursting with well-being, charismatic star of an international organization broadcasting services worldwide, hangs out with Oprah. (see page 158)

Timothy Leary

World-renown poster boy for mind-expansion through the use of psychedelic drugs, considered drug use a spiritual search. (see page 116)

Yogananda

The first celebrity guru, welcomed everywhere, by heads of state, celebrities. (see page 44)

AFTERWORD

And so, our tour must come to an end, for now. As with all works of this kind, there will be inadvertent omissions, obvious errors, and things that just plain piss people off. In this book I have chosen to focus on spiritual groups that were either born in L.A. or have had a significant enough presence here to warrant a national or international effect. If my choices offend, I apologize in advance. That said, I welcome any and all comments, suggestions, arguments, pointing out of what I left out, and, of course, praise. Corrections will be made as needed in future revisions of the book.

Please contact me at
info@catherineauman.com

If you would like to leave a book review on Amazon, that would be most appreciated.

Happy Travels, both inner and out!

ABOUT THE AUTHOR

Catherine with Timothy Leary (1990)

Catherine Auman is a Licensed Marriage and Family Therapist (LMFT) in private practice and the Founder and Director of The Transpersonal Counseling Center. Catherine appears frequently on podcasts, radio, and TV, and she is a popular speaker and workshop leader. Her writings have been published online and in journals, magazines, and books in the U.S. and Europe.

Catherine began her search early. During childhood and adolescence, she read widely in mythology, literature and philosophy. She began studying meditation and yoga in 1972, astrology in 1980, and entered a graduate transpersonal (spiritual) psychology program in 1983. Along the way she has explored and dived deeply into a wide variety of spiritual and personal growth paths including Eastern religions, Ken Wilbur's Integral Theory, 12-step programs, entheogens, NLP, and bodywork. Catherine became a sannyasin of Osho in 1985 and was given the name Ma Dhyan Shaida ("intoxicated with love"). She lived for a year at the Osho ashram in India, a full-time immersion in tantra and meditation. Catherine lives in Los Angeles with her husband, Greg Lawrence, with whom she teaches tantra and relationship enhancement.

Visit her online at **catherineauman.com**
Facebook: www.facebook.com/catherineaumanlmft
Instagram: @catherineauman
YouTube: www.YouTube.com/c/catherineauman

ACKNOWLEDGMENTS

Thanks to:

All my friends who asked me, "How do you know all this stuff? You should write it down."

Maja D'Aoust, the White Witch, whose 2010 tour for Esotouric got me thinking this spiritual stuff would make a good book.

Karenlin Madoff, without whose ongoing enthusiasm for the progress updates I shared during our weekly walk 'n squawks, this book would never have seen completion.

My readers, Sandra Sloss Giedeman and Margaret Drewry Walsh, talented poets and authors whose work I recommend you check out.

Greg Lawrence, my husband, who much to my amazement early on in our relationship thought it was a great date to go photograph many of the locations in this book.

Philip Goldberg and Felicia Tomasko of *LA Yoga Magazine* for their permission to use Philip's wonderful piece as the Foreword.

My sister, Lauren Walker Lee, who is a champion of everything I write. I look forward to reading your book someday.

Katrina Pacheco, whose creative genius made our collaboration such fun, and for turning my photos into mini-works of art.

To all the misfits, eccentrics, freaks, explorers, dreamers, believers, out-on-a-limb-ers, psychics, rebels, badasses, disturbers of the status quo, kids who were picked on in school, weirdos, and the non-pretty who came to L.A. to make something of yourselves – Welcome! This is your town.

And most heartfelt thanks to L.A., our beloved City of the Angels, for your radiance, your endless opportunity, and your crazy amalgam of the sacred and the profane.

INDEX

Adi Da Samraj 5, 54

Aetherius Society 35, 38, 50-51, 53

Agape International Spiritual Center 141, 142, 158-159, 230

Angelus Temple 35, 69-71, 79

Anger, Kenneth 82, 87, 89, 92

Autobiography of a Yogi 1, 44, 51

Azusa Street Revival 73

B.O.T.A. 87, 90-91

Babalon Working 87, 88, 234

Beckwith, Michael Bernard 141, 158-159, 239

Berg, Philip and Karen 144

Bhaktifest 5, 167, 222

Bikram Yoga 150-151, 223, 234

Blavatsky, Helena Petrovna 63-65

Bonnie Brae House 35, 72-73, 80, 230

Botánicas 29-30, 139

Budapest, Zsuzsanna 124-125, 236

Buddhafield, The 130-131

Cabot's Pueblo Museum 174, 190-191

Cameron, Marjorie 82, 85, 87, 88-89, 92, 236, 238

Case, Paul Foster 82, 87, 90

Castaneda, Carlos 109, 121-123, 234, 238

Cathedral of Our Lady of the Angels 99, 228, 230

Catholic Church 26, 29-30, 95-96, 235

Children of God 114-115, 223

Choudhury, Bikram 3, 150-151, 223, 234

Chumash 8, 10, 14,17, 19, 135, 205, 206-207, 209, 222, 223, 233

Chumash Cultural Center 19, 200

Church of Scientology 35, 38, 40-43, 92, 223, 234

Church of Synanon 126-127

Cleargreen, Inc. 123

Cleveland, James 119

Colton, Ann Ree 164-165, 237

Crouch, Andraé 119-120

Crouch, Sandra 119-120

Crowley, Aleister 82, 83, 85, 86-87, 88-89, 93

D'Aoust, Maja 83, 245

Desert Christ Park 172, 188-189

Devi, Indra 2, 166

Devil's Gate 93

Feminist Wicca 109, 124-125

Festival of the Chariots 161, 169

First African Methodist Episcopal (AME) Church of Los Angeles 97, 99

Flirty Fishing 114-115, 237

Giant Rock 52, 171, 178-179, 180, 182, 232

Goodman, Trudy 147

Gospel music 118-120

Hall, Manly P. 65, 66, 82, 235

Hare Krishnas 3, 109, 160-162

Holmes, Ernest 140-141

Holy Hell 130-131, 223

Hubbard, L. Ron 41, 42, 85, 87, 88, 93, 234, 239

Huffington, Arianna 153, 154-155

Huxley, Aldous 2, 54-57, 116, 238

Huxley, Laura 54, 57

Inn of the Seventh Ray 135-136

InsightLA 147

Integratron 171, 175, 176-177, 180

International Centers of Divine Awakening (ICODA) 163

Islam in L.A. 106-107

Judaism in L.A. 103-105

Joshua Tree 181, 182-183, 232
Joshua Tree Retreat Center 37, 171, 186-187
Kabbalah Center 109, 142, 144-145
King, Dr. George 51
Kirtan 166-167
Knight, Leonard 195-198, 223
Krishnamurti 2, 57, 64-65, 85, 209-210
Krotona Apartments 39, 61-62
Krotona Institute 35, 61-62, 65, 207, 209-210
Kuruvugna Springs 13, 110
Leary, Timothy 56, 116-117, 182, 239, 243
Lake Shrine 1, 109, 228, 230
Leek, Sybil 83
Lemuria, lost continent of 8
Lessing, Edith Maida 74-75, 237
Lizard people 76
Markland, Ted 182-183
McPherson, Aimee Semple 35, 69-71, 80, 135, 168, 220, 223, 234, 236, 238
Meditation Mount 207, 210
Mindful Awareness Research Center (MARC) 147
Miss Velma 220-221, 237
Mission San Fernando Rey de Espana 28
Mission San Gabriel Arcangel 25-27
Mission Santa Barbara, Old 200, 230, 233
Monastery of the Angels 35, 39, 58-59, 230, 237
Mount Baldy 192, 194
Mount Helios Love Cult 74-75
Movement of Spiritual Inner Awareness (MSIA) 128-129, 152, 154, 156, 234
Native Peoples 9-23
New Age Movement 139
New Thought Movement 138, 159
Niscience 164-165
Ojai 2, 17, 61, 209-211, 232
Parsons, Jack 83, 84-85, 87, 88, 92-93, 223, 234, 239
Peace Awareness Labyrinth and Gardens 81, 129, 152-153, 228
Pentecostal Movement 35, 72-73, 118
Philosophical Research Society (PRS) 35, 66-67, 80
Premodaya, Swami 163
Protestants 96
Puvunga 14, 21, 214
Reese, Della 120
Regardie, Israel 83, 87
Religious Science, Church of 138, 140-141
Righter, Carroll 35, 83
Salvation Mountain 193, 195-198
Satanic Temple 93
Science of Mind 138, 140-141
Self-Realization Fellowship 1, 35, 44-49, 79, 217, 228, 230
Serra, Junipero 27
Seymour, William J. 72
Shaktifest 167, 222
Shalawa Meadow 17, 203, 204-205
Source Family 39, 112-113
Spellbound Sky 80-81, 227
St. Vabiana's 102
Stark, Jen 117
Swami's Café 217-218
Templo Santa Muerte 93
The Secret Teachings of All Ages 66
Theosophy 2, 51, 61-65, 85, 135, 138, 164, 174, 191, 209-210

Thunderbolt Books 110, 227, 230
Tongva 10, 19, 21, 23, 26-27, 93, 194
Tongva Park 13-14, 110
Toypurina 22-23, 27, 236
UFOs 36, 52-53, 175, 178-179, 181, 182
University of Santa Monica (USM) 67, 129, 156-157
Van Tassel, George 178-179, 180
Vedanta Temple 2, 3, 35, 38, 54-55, 57, 227, 230
Venice 168-169
Vortexes 35, 36-37, 38, 53, 58, 72, 171, 175, 181, 186-187, 200, 206, 210, 232-233,
Wayfarer's Chapel 212-213, 215, 229
Western Gate, The 17, 203, 206-207
Williamson, Marianne 148-149, 236, 239
Winston, Diana 147
Wishtoyo Chumash Village 13
Yoga West 133, 142
Yogananda, Paramahansa 1, 3, 44-49, 166, 217, 223, 230, 235, 239
YogaWorks 3, 166
Yogi Bhajan 4, 132-133, 235
Zaca Lake 17, 233

OTHER BOOKS BY GREEN TARA PRESS

At Green Tara Press, we are dedicated to publishing works that promote compassion, healing and love, and awaken and inspire readers to enlightened action. We share the tantric vision that all is sacred. Visit us online at **www.greentarapress.com**

Books

In This Hour, by Sandra Sloss Giedeman

I-Stretch & Strengthen: The Take-Everywhere Exercise System by Bob Alonzi

Journaling as Sacred Practice: An Act of Extreme Bravery, by Cynthia Gregory

On Summer Solstice Road, by Jerry Garcia

Really Truly, by Holly Prado

Rim of the World Highway, by Margaret Drewry Walsh

Shortcuts to Mindfulness: 100 Ways to Personal and Spiritual Growth, by Catherine Auman, LMFT

Tantric Dating: Bringing Love and Awareness to the Dating Process by Catherine Auman, LMFT

Relaxation and Meditation Audios

Awareness Breathing, by Catherine Auman, LMFT

Deeply Relaxed, by Catherine Auman, LMFT

Tantric Embodiment Induction, by Catherine Auman, LMFT